Therapy

Intimacy Between Strangers

Don Feasey

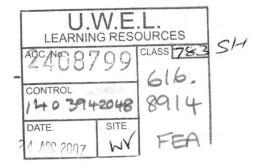

palgrave
macmillan

First published 2005 by
PALGRAVE MACMILLAN
Houndmills, Basingstoke, Hampshire RG21 6XS and
175 Fifth Avenue, New York, N.Y. 10010
Companies and representatives throughout the world

PALGRAVE MACMILLAN is the global academic imprint of the Palgrave Macmillan division of St. Martin's Press, LLC and of Palgrave Macmillan Ltd. Macmillan® is a registered trademark in the United States, United Kingdom and other countries. Palgrave is a registered trademark in the European Union and other countries.

ISBN-13: 978–1–4039–4204–3 paperback
ISBN-10: 1–4039–4204–8 paperback

This book is printed on paper suitable for recycling and made from fully managed and sustained forest sources.

A catalogue record for this book is available from the British Library.

A catalog record for this book is available from the Library of Congress.

10   9   8   7   6   5   4   3   2   1
14   13   12   11   10   09   08   07   06   05

Printed in China

Grateful thanks to Jeanne for all her help in preparing this book. Remembering all my clients of now and the past, in therapy and supervision.

Contents

Acknowledgements

I wish to express my thanks to Andrew McAleer at Palgrave Macmillan for his encouragement in seeing this book through to production.

The author and publishers would like to thank Craig Newnes, editor of the *Journal of Critical Psychology, Counselling and Psychotherapy* (formerly *Changes* journal), for permission to reproduce Chapters 4 and 6.

Note on Confidentiality

Readers will note that in the text of this book I speak about the inviolate nature of the psychotherapeutic relationship. In other words, what a client discloses in the therapy room is not passed on to another person or body without the express wish of the client. In certain extreme circumstances this rule will not be observed. Usually it is when issues of self-harm or harm to others arises in such as manner as to constitute a palpable threat to the client, to the therapist or to another.

To the author of a book such as mine this situation represents a real challenge. The nub of it is how to present experiential material drawn from clients' lives without betraying the identity and confidence of the client. The reality of the scope of this book virtually makes it impossible to rely upon getting the permission of all my clients past and present to use material, to which they might attribute to themselves. In other words, someone may say 'That is me he is writing about!' and feel offended or betrayed.

I have been in practice as a therapist for over twenty years and in this time I have encountered a vast range of human experience in my therapy room, and in the process have found ways of working with my clients to their psychotherapeutic advantage. This book sets out to use this experience and take it beyond my practice to a wider range of readership. To illustrate my approach to therapy I have of necessity to use the work that has been processed in my therapy room with the individuals and couples I have worked with.

To do this I have devised a method of description of what may be called 'general therapeutic experience' presented through fictionalised individual therapeutic descriptions. I give a name to the fictionalised client for the purpose of illustration, to personalise the account. I provide within the description human experience that is particular to the case being described, but common to the body of my psychotherapy practice. To engage the reader I dramatise the material to put it in the context of the everyday lives of human beings. So if a former client reads this book and feels identified with the material I describe then I am not surprised. We all identify with accounts of human experience, good or bad, happy or despairing; it is part of the human condition.

Most of the examples I use in this book are drawn from relationships with clients of the past. However, this is not always the case. I introduce fictional descriptions to ensure that others cannot identify a person in an individual and particular way. Sometimes I use the change of gender, social circumstance, place and time, to distance any of my past clients from being placed in the position of being identified and associated with the 'example' I am providing. Sometimes readers may recognise aspects of the 'story' as belonging to themselves. That aspect may belong to many other readers including myself or members of my family, friends and colleagues.

Throughout this text I have used the term 'example' to indicate material that has been drawn together in the way described above, where it has been drawn from a whole range of relationships and is not in the sole possession of any single individual except the fictitious named client.

I discussed this issue in some depth with my wife who is a writer. She responded with the following anecdote. She was attending a writers workshop and had just finished reading aloud a description of a male character that featured in a short story. As she finished, a member of the writers group cried out, 'Oh, I know that man, I know him.' My wife replied, 'No, you do not know this man – I have just invented him!'

D.F.

Introduction

'It's basically a sort of difficulty in seeing other people as people . . . because you can't grasp the fact that they have their own internal life.'
   'So they're objects?'
   'Yes.'

                              (Pat Barker, *Double Vision*, 2003)

No one can tolerate a too intimate approach to his neighbour.
                     (attributed to Freud in Luepnitz, 2003)

Client-centred therapy. Its central hypothesis is that the growthful potential of any individual will tend to be released in a relationship in which the helping person is experiencing and communicating realness, caring and a deeply sensitive non-judgmental understanding. *

                              (Meador & Rogers, 1972)

This book is not intended to be a formal textbook and its scholarship is limited. It is primarily intended to be an examination of my work as a psychoanalytic psychotherapist for some twenty years. In those years certain experiences have emerged for me as central to the good practice of psychotherapy and therapeutic counselling and I wish to share them with tolerant readers, who I hope will benefit from the effort of reading this book. As a result I have written in an informal style, revealing personal and anecdotal material to the scrutiny of readers whom I beg to be patient. I have taken care not to hurt or expose others by my frankness. But there will be a loss to those who look for a formal didactic style of writing and the presence of a host of references to be trawled through, to check the accuracy of my remarks. I believe that most of my readers are likely to be informed and 'canny', quite capable of judging the merits of my arguments and assertions.

*   Here the term 'helping person' is used, rather than the term 'counsellor' or 'therapist'. In this book when I use the term 'therapist' I intend to include any practitioner of psychotherapy or therapeutic counselling, from whatever school or discipline. When I use the term 'psychoanalytic psychotherapist' then it is obvious that it is meant exclusively.

In these twenty years much has changed in the world of personal psychotherapy and counselling. When I started in private practice and as a part-time therapist in the NHS in Salford I was a pretty rare bird. Carl Rogers (1967) was on the scene but the growth industry of counselling was still to emerge. Clinical psychologists and psychiatrists regarded psychoanalytic psychotherapists with deep suspicion. That was a long time ago but the tension still exists and both sides tend to be on the defensive. I think, too, that classical psychoanalysts, mostly found in London, simply regarded us with disdain. Readers will probably know that the professional organisation of psychoanalysts withdrew from their original collaboration with the United Kingdom Council for Psychotherapy, when they were denied a final right of veto on collectively agreed decisions. As for the army of counsellors that now exist, they seem to prefer to stay on their own side of the fence as far as disputes about ideology are concerned – not so much disputing with psychotherapists as ignoring them. I meet with some experienced and sophisticated counsellors for supervision and we talk with great ease, sharing as we do many professional attitudes in common. But they are exceptional. For the most part, I rarely meet counsellors and play no part in that expanding enterprise.

However, in spite of all these difficulties, back in Salford twenty years ago there were clients looking for therapy. Within the local catchment area, where a small NHS experimental day therapeutic community served the locality, and in the more rarefied atmosphere of a small city in the north of England, there were people looking for therapy. In both my home area, as it was then, and the city of Salford, the population was poorly served with facilities or staff for psychotherapy and there were great gaps in provision, and these gaps still remain today. In many parts of the UK, especially in rural areas, there is virtually no provision of psychotherapy. Nevertheless the situation has improved and hopefully will continue to do so.

So to begin at the beginning
(Dylan Thomas, *Under Milkwood*)

A therapy appointment is made, often by telephone. Little may be known in advance about the nature of the person who is to become the 'client', but sometimes, as in the case given below, she may be known in part to the therapist. In reality it may be an expected call. However, little is known about the encounter that is about to take place. Although a ritual of meeting may be put in place by the therapist, the ritual does not and cannot forecast the nature of the therapeutic encounter. The therapist and the client must be prepared for anything. Both must always be ready to be surprised, pleased, disappointed, dismayed, angry, interested, alienated. Sometimes the meeting may be well rehearsed by the client and established from previous therapeutic encounters with the therapist; I will go on merely to add that there is usually an undercurrent of active curiosity on both sides of the encounter.

From this very early position of awareness I wish to move forward in my thinking to the main plank of my therapeutic position, both clinically and ethically. The therapist waiting upon the client needs to position herself in a space, which Rogers (1967) described as a position of 'unconditional regard'. How can anyone quarrel with this assertion? The problem is that it does not go far enough in examining the human condition of the therapist as well as the client. As Anna Sands (2000) writes:

> In any case unconditional acceptance will extend only as far as the therapist can extend himself. The work will be limited by the character, motivation and potential of both client and practitioner. So there is nothing unconditional about it.

The psychoanalytic view would suggest that the mind is dynamic and in possession of waves of sometimes complementary and sometimes oppositional states of being, which come into play upon the position of waiting. These states of being are sometimes conscious and sometimes unconscious.

Although the conscious intention is to greet the coming client with 'unconditional regard', the reality is that all therapists will, in such circumstances, begin to frame the coming client in response to internal conscious and unconscious formulations. These responses will have been stimulated by receiving a phone call or letter. Recently I received a long letter from a distraught husband describing his wife's emotional and social difficulties and asking me to let him know if I thought I was the person who could work with her therapeutically. This, I would add, is a very rare occurrence. I won't describe the detail of my response but I knew immediately that he had touched on feelings of hate inside myself. I am not sure at this moment which was the main figure of hate. Did I hate him for this controlling and manipulative approach? Did I hate his wife for colluding with this move on his part? Did I hate them as a couple? Even now as I write I am not sure. When she came to see me I adopted an outward conscious position of *acceptance and respect*. This I regard as a technical accomplishment derived from my early training and subsequent practice. What was more important for me was to place myself in a psychological position of intense self-observation. I could then move into a *relational position* of communication with this client on her first visit. I have always valued the position of Harry Stack Sullivan (1953) when he set out the view that the interpersonal is always the imperative in the meeting between human beings. And this view should surely apply to therapist and client.

What might result from not being available to a client in a relational therapeutic stance, especially in the early stages of a relationship, is illustrated by a fragment of an unpublished case study I wrote many years ago.

Fragment

Of . . . 'X', a psychoanalyst, whom she had seen twice a week for eighteen months, she said: '*I can't remember her name and in any case I wouldn't talk to her about family relationships.*'

H. [my client] described the woman as Middle European and: '*Very cold, in her early thirties: she smoked and sat with her eyes closed; she was quite impenetrable.*'

The analyst didn't say very much, was experienced as remote and formal. At the end of the relationship Ms. H. wished to: '*block her out of my mind. I wanted to escape her – but I felt guilty.*'

Significantly, just before leaving London in 1992 she found another woman therapist who was '*the first therapist who really understood me*'.

This first punitive therapeutic relationship was brought to a close when the client left her post in a large southern city for professional advancement and moved to the north where she entered my consulting room and my care. At this stage I clearly needed to pay a good deal of attention to building a fruitful therapeutic alliance. Sitting with eyes closed and a cold and distant manner was not going to help at all. On the contrary, I had to take heed of the fact that my client had 'lost' a trusted woman therapist who was being exchanged for an unknown man. Inside myself I felt quite capable of meeting these conditions and I was aware of a feeling of anger that my profession of psychotherapy had, in the first instance, been experienced so punitively. I felt a positive desire to offer something much better in the form of a therapeutic relationship.

I was certainly not going to accept and practise the orthodox psychoanalytic stance advocated by Freud, that is: 'The doctor should be opaque to his patients, and, like a mirror, should show then nothing but what is shown to him.' My own opinion is that the presence of this position in psychoanalysis is because the therapist is governed by fear – fear of sex and intimacy. I am glad to say that after such a challenging and unpromising beginning, the client, after about 18 months of work with me, moved back to the south into a settled relationship with a man and a good job with further professional advancement.

Some psychotherapists and counsellors will recognise my use of the term 'relational'. It is used among a limited number of therapists in this country although the 'relational approach' has a much stronger following in the USA (see Mitchell, 1988, 1995). The meaning of the term 'relational' when applied to the word 'transference' in psychoanalytical circles implies offering the client a more available therapeutic presence by the therapist than may be offered by more formally trained psychotherapists and psychoanalysts. It is a thought-out presence, responsive to the nature of the client. It takes into account the observed needs of the client especially in terms of their presented communication processes. It certainly does not disown the need for the therapist to remain alert to transference issues in the developing psychotherapeutic relationship. I must admit it has taken me some time to move towards this position and like others I am still exploring its possibilities.

In general, the reader will detect the strong presence of Sigmund Freud in this book and this is because, although I recognise there has been much revision, elaboration and exploration of early Freudian concepts, it is also quite obvious that the genius of the man is still active today (see Freud, 1962). This is true even when contemporary counsellors and therapists do not recognise the source of their current ideas and practice.

Then there is the matter of language. In this book I will use technical, academic language sparingly. An interesting article in the *Guardian* newspaper took up the matter of academic language in a pretty forceful way. I think much theoretical psychoanalytic language has become stultifyingly academic and I welcomed the *Guardian* article by Ophelia Benson (2003). She describes some academic language as: 'the notoriously opaque, preening, self-admiring, inflated prose of "theory" '. She was actually referring to the language of critical literary theory, and holding an MA in Modern Literature I could not agree with her more. I identified her criticism with much contemporary writing on psychoanalytical theory. The result of such scholarship is to hold ideas about analysis very firmly in the grip of a small elite group of discussants, and at the same time move it away from the plain language that any layman may employ to achieve a clear understanding of the issues under discussion.

My style is intended to be approachable and informal, and I hope to invest the telling of the book with emotional energy as well as preserving a sense of professional accuracy. I know I will on occasion be polemical, but if the reader doesn't agree with me then patience will be called for. No one has to agree with me! Disagreement is welcome. Some psychoanalytic language I find exhausted and unhelpful – indeed sometimes completely objectionable. I shall not talk about 'objects' (meaning other human beings) or 'part-objects' (meaning aspects of another person). I shall try to observe a properly respectful stance towards the nature of humanity in this book and look for other words that convey the same meaning. I espouse the notion of the interpersonal and regard its rediscovery in our own time as important as we try to make sense and manage our interpersonal relationships. Freud too, especially in his early writings, took into account the importance of feelings towards those in social relation with us, as well as the presence of intrapsychic experience.

Unlike Melanie Klein (1932) I shall not speculate about the earliest activity of the mind in the newly born child. We know now the baby's brain goes on growing and developing after birth. Consequently, it is a matter of guesswork as to what the process of thought and feeling consists of at birth. The early Freudian suggestion of pleasure and unpleasure and the instinctual need to find nourishment in food and the presence of a prime carer, still rings true for me as a father of four children. The great danger is that in observing the newly born child we simply project our own feelings towards the child. For example, if it cries, because of discomfort or pain or hunger, then its urgent demands make us feel uneasy, anxious, helpless, depressed and even angry. These feelings are all too easily placed upon the child who is in no position to negotiate or reject the experience. I would urge all readers to watch carefully the next Punch and Judy show they see on an English summer beach, holding entranced the attention of an audience of very young children. See what happens to the 'damned baby' and ponder its meaning. Working with my wife in raising four children and experiencing the multitude of feelings we both encountered in the process, continuing to this present day, has convinced me there are no formulaic answers to the mystery of birth and growth. I find it unbelievable that children enter the world with an organised emotional world active within the interior of their mind. It is my view that, for most part, we have to learn in a dynamic process of both conscious and unconscious activity, involving the world around us. In therapy we try to pursue the meaning of these complex experiences and relate that understanding to our need to live fruitful, satisfactory and, hopefully, happy lives. Hence my advocacy of the 'relational approach', which challenges the abstractions, language, the theatrical speculations and techniques of Kleinian theory.

I would like to end this Introduction by using some material provided by a client many years ago. She was capable, intelligent and committed to both her professional work in marketing and her therapy. One of her central problems was struggling to manage the intense emotional feelings that arose within her, accompanying almost every close relationship she had, with either men or women or, in this instance, children. She was very interested in children, especially girl children around the ages of seven or eight. She knew children in this age group and she would visit and play with them. One day, somewhat distressed, she came for her appointment and handed me a copy of an exchange she had had with one of the children concerned, her niece. I reproduce some of the wording here, in edited form to protect their privacy:

> *What do you feel about us Aunty? . . .*
> *Why don't you just play with one of us? . . .*
> *Are you upset about it all? . . .*
> *Do you mind about it? . . .*
> *Do you wish it hadn't come to this? . . .*
> *You used to play with me all the time. . . .*
> *You don't have to play with me any more. . . .*

I hope the readers of this book find this communication as touching as I do. It provides vivid evidence of the part that quite raw emotion plays within the personal relationships of everyday life, as experienced by a young girl. Although struggling with her language skills, the level of emotional expression of insight into the relationship with my client is impressive and moving. She is speaking entirely at the level of feeling and empathy. I think it is reassuring to psychotherapists that we are working in such a significant and important area of human existence. This letter validates many of the concerns that arise when working with our clients. I am indebted to this child in her profound and innocent observation. Much important material emerged within the therapy room as a result of this encounter between caring adult and child.

This book, then, is devoted to exploring the relationship between therapist and client and its sub-title is intended to raise the matter in a challenging and speculative manner. The context of this discussion is my own experience of working with human beings in therapy in a number of different and contrasting situations. Some of the material comes from the relatively secure and privileged milieu of my private consulting room, and some from

the rougher, tougher world of a NHS day centre, run along therapeutic lines. In each instance I have attempted to treat my clients (or patients as they were described in the NHS) with equal respect and interest (although to be frank some clients/patients are more interesting than others).

The Essence of Therapy: Janice and Craig

Example

I glanced at the clock. 10:55 a.m. She would arrive at any moment now. Sure enough the bell rang; an abrupt piercing command. As I walked down the hall I had a vision in my mind of her leaning casually, detached, cool and remote against the pillar of the doorway. I opened the door. There she was. She gave me the merest of glances and moved forward. I lurched to one side to let her pass. Not a sound from either of us. No greeting or acknowledgement, just movement, movement with purpose. I pointed and she opened the door to my therapy room. I murmured my usual greeting mantra about being with her shortly. It is my customary practice to leave clients alone for a moment or two to settle themselves and to 'take in' their surroundings.

I went into our sitting room and tidied up some newspapers and cushions. I looked at my wife who was reading the morning Guardian. *'I'm starting now.' She gave a short glance and a small grunt of acknowledgement and I left the room.*

Janice was sitting in her usual position, looking out of the window. She made no move to acknowledge my entry. Her body was quite immobile. I looked at her with a deliberate focus of eye and head gesture. She made no response. She sat, removed, detached, upright and poised. Her posture and appearance invited notice. She looked as if she was in command. There was nothing improvised about her appearance, the whole image was of self-possession; rehearsed and deliberate. Today she was dressed in a smart suit, grey with a faint white stripe; the jacket was fitted, the skirt straight, ending just above the knee. It was an expensive garment. Janice invariably wore formal clothes for her sessions with me. Maybe with others as well. Who knows? These clothes spoke of money and control, a certain kind of dignity and repose – they belied her status as a young woman barely twenty years old, a student at the university. In the silence I would

10

*invariably try to understand the communication of her presence.
It appeared I was to expect a silent hour.*

*I mumbled another greeting which she ignored. She always
would. I lapsed into silence with her. I anticipated that this was
going to be a tortuous hour but I had learned from her that to sit
with her in the silence was what she wanted, what she came for.
She came once a week, always on time. But today I had a surprise
for her.*

Janice, age 20, had come to me privately by referral from a psychiatric psychotherapy department. It read as follows: 'Janice X was a
patient in this unit from Y to Z. Today she has been discharged.'
John, a psychiatrist I knew well, a man of some repute, psychoanalytical in orientation and experienced in both working with
groups and individuals, signed the letter. His was an exceptional
unit. I was perturbed by this angry referral letter, but thought it
better not to pursue the matter with him. On discharge Janice had
overdosed very severely and ended up in intensive care in our local
hospital. On recovery she had been discharged to me for
psychotherapy via a counselling service at the university. Janice
had presented herself, quite voluntarily, a few weeks before this
session and openly negotiated a fee, attendance requirements and
a 'no harm' agreement with me without any difficulty. After the
practical matters had been settled she lapsed into silence.

*And now I was experiencing the silence again in all its oppres-
siveness. I had made an observation, passed a comment and even
attempted an interpretation. There had been no response. I had
decided to hold the silence with her for about fifteen minutes at a
time and then speak to her using my emotional understanding of
the experience as my guide. But there had been no evident
response. Her body language had hardly changed at all; she did
not speak or look at me. The session passed. Remarkably quickly.
Ten minutes before the moment of closure approached she began
to make one or two restless movements in her chair, very small,
hardly detectable but certainly present. Now came my surprise.
'Janice,' I said, 'I have been thinking about you and our relationship and I think it would help us a lot if you came to see me
more frequently, say three times a week, Monday, Wednesday and
Friday at the same time, if you can manage it. What do you*

think about my proposal? I would like you to think about it. We can discuss it, if you wish, over the next few weeks.' Her movements stopped. She appeared to freeze, sitting in a still silence, but now it had a different quality. Then she looked straight at me and spoke.

'OK, that is fine. Do we start next week? How much more shall I have to pay you?'

'You know my scale. How much can you afford?' I replied.

She named a figure and I nodded. 'Are you sure that you can afford as much as that.'

'You would do better to ask John, my father,' she replied with a soft snigger.

'I would prefer you paid me from your own money. Do you want to discuss this change any further? Perhaps we should.'

Now I knew that there had been two Johns in her life.

She made no reply, stood up and headed for the door.

'See you on Monday then.'

She briefly grinned at me, baring her teeth, and was gone. I felt no comfort in her grin. It had a savage character about it.

My proposal had come out of my own frustration with the situation I found myself in with this client. I had come across 'silent' clients before but never one who was so determinedly closed and resistant to all my attempts at communication. I became exasperated too, but this feeling gave me a clue as to how to proceed. I decided my approach should be paradoxical. Instead of regarding the client as untreatable and terminating the relationship, I decided to attempt another approach where my commitment to my client would be demonstrated. I would ask her to come more often. It seemed that by following my intuitive response to the situation I had done the right thing. Or so it seemed at the time.

Monday morning at precisely 10:00 a.m. the doorbell rang. Janice was again at the doorstep. This time not leaning against the frame but standing still and four square in the doorway. I stepped back murmuring a soft 'Good morning.' She followed me into the hall and went without prompting into the therapy room.

I took my time following her, expecting a change. I anticipated a shift in her demeanour. There was none. She sat as usual looking out of the window, upright and posed. Again she was formally dressed. Not a glance came towards me: no recognition of my presence. I decided to speak. And then I decided not to speak, and then to speak, and then not to speak. But what to speak about? My training came to my rescue. I thought, 'Yes, I will speak but I will simply speak about the confusion in my mind.' And so I did.

'You know, I feel as if I am an actor in some rather arty French film. In fact, as if we both are. You know the kind of thing, all shadows, silences and a cello playing softly in the background. What is to be made of it all? The audience is left to its own conclusions.' I paused but in such a manner as to suggest I would continue.

'The confusion rests in the silence.'

She broke in: 'There is no need to say anything, I come and that is enough.'

Her face was momentarily alive. Her eyes lost the dull absence. She twisted her body a fraction further away from me.

Janice had acted disruptively in the therapeutic community. She had taken a small group of patients off to the local pub and poured scorn on the therapists, the regime and, particularly, John the consultant psychotherapist.

The memory of this flashed into my mind and after a pause I retorted: 'Perhaps you sit there in silence rubbishing me, rubbishing the therapy and particularly rubbishing yourself for being here at all.'

She made no reply but her body moved slightly as if she had suffered a small sting.

I could never have anticipated these scenes before meeting Janice. There is a stereotypical view of the silent therapist and the reflecting patient/client, which is common to the lay person's account of psychoanalytic psychotherapy, but the silent client is quite another thing. Although I had encountered silence before in the therapy room I had never before met it in such totality before meeting Janice. However, the issue is not so much that of what to do with silence, as one of adopting a psychological posture of creative and flexible psychotherapeutic response to whatever occurs in the therapy room. After all, she might have turned out to be a non-stop talker. The literature on the subject of silence is sparse. Folland (1994) confirms this as he works on a postgraduate dissertation in psychotherapy:

> One is struck by the paucity of writings on this dimension of human language in relation to the weight of material devoted to speech – its practical and theoretical postulations.

To help his readers think about the subject Folland (1994) writes:

> In the beginning there is silence. When two people meet for the first time the initial silence of their internal biographies is matched by an exterior silence prior to an exchange of greetings.

He then goes on to structure his discussion under four headings. In the first instance silence is identified as resistance to psychoanalytical psychotherapy, which needs to be overcome. For the second Folland draws attention to the meditational character of silence, easily accommodated in religious practice where it is regarded as communication, but not easily accommodated in the 'talking therapies' where such silence is often described as pathological. In the third it is described as a manipulative manoeuvre where the therapist is forced to 'wait' (as with the instance of late coming). The fourth view Folland traces back to Khan, who explored the notion of silence as being an interpersonal experience between the therapist and her client in which the client is actively describing the nature of a former relationship where damage had occurred and depression had resulted. In other words, the silence is active with meaning. A comparison might be drawn between such silence and Edvard Munch's famous painting *The Scream*. Paintings can be seen but not heard, at least not by the ear. The eye has to do the 'listening'.

This view contains the essence of what this book is about: it explores and advocates the creation of a creative and imaginative relationship between the client and the therapist where each responds to the presence of the other without conventional or restrictive institutional intervention. The aim is, as always, to understand and this applies to both client and therapist who need to understand one another, and every effort has to be made to overcome anything that impedes that progress. Therefore, sometimes to pathologise the silence of the client is merely to reinforce the silence, leaving it located in a place that becomes inaccessible to both client and therapist alike.

The relationship with Janice soon revealed deep deprivational wounds and Oedipal confusion of a destructive nature, especially in relation to her mother, which the silence demonstrated in her holding back from me in the early days of therapy. The holding back at first seemed to me simply to be resentful anger, but eventually I came to see and experience it as a far more complex state, as feelings began to emerge about a conspiratorial and collusive relationship she had held with John, her father. The two of them often mounted both symbolic and realistic attacks on her mother, with the aim of humiliating and denigrating her, which they succeeded in doing. To complicate things the father would often treat Janice like a favourite male slave. He was especially pleased to use her as a chauffeuse of his Jaguar car and she was often sent to the local airport to receive important business guests. There were marked sexual tensions between them. Of course, nothing was ever acknowledged between father, mother and daughter concerning this dysfunctional family scene. Everything was acted-out in a kind of familial silence. A silence that was oppressive and all-enveloping. Janice reproduced this stance in the therapy room where it became a source of dialogue as the weeks went by. So we spoke about the silence and the silence was gradually revealed for what it was – a noisy, intruding, controlling presence.

Janice worked with me for three years while she was studying for her degree. She left my care, I thought rather prematurely, to go to the South and start a professional training course. This did not surprise me – in fact, I thought it quite appropriate. About three years later she wrote and suggested she come back for more work, and did for about another two years. In this period her main aim seemed to attempt to establish healthy relationships with men, turning away from sadism and masochism in favour of sexual affection and intimacy. She was more open, sometimes sarcastic, her own foolishness being the butt of her humour – now much more deeply engaged in a conscious sense than before. I felt pleased and relieved that the early struggles had been worthwhile and I had not made too much a mess of things in attempting to achieve a working relationship with her. Therapists, all of us, need reassurance of the validity of our work. We are human.

Another example

More recently I have been working with another young person, a young professional man called Craig. He is very intelligent and well educated. But in his early days of therapy his silence was not total, but to some extent even more frustrating because he would start a sentence and after a few words stop, often leaving the sentence without a subject, its grammatical structure in ruins. When this happened, as it did quite often, he would wring his hands in what appeared to be an act of desperation and despair. But some readers may quite legitimately say, 'This latter reflection of yours is mere projection. It was your desperation and despair that you were experiencing, not his.' And there is more than an ounce of truth in this comment. I found these incomplete sentences very, very difficult to deal with. In some ways absolute silence was easier. On the other hand his body language was very expressive, paradoxically noisy. It could not be ignored and his pain was evident. I exercised personal supervision in these sessions in order to monitor my own pain and frustration at experiencing his evident suffering. Then came a breakthrough. It came when I attempted an interpretation of this behaviour as anger. He stirred from his introspective examining and retorted quickly that what I said was wrong, and that it was not helping him. He wanted me to wait and let him find his own voice. I agreed without hesitation. I did suggest, however, that we move to a twice-weekly regime and he fairly readily agreed. He never failed to come and gradually the communication between us began to occur more openly, coherently and actively, despite occasional lapses into silence and hand wringing.

These two examples are given because they challenge two contrasting means of working with clients who withhold in the therapy or counselling situation. The classic psychoanalytic frame would encourage a distance on the part of the therapist, the silence would be as much a part of the therapist's stance as the client's. A tentatively applied 'person centred' reflection of empathetic feeling did nothing for either of these clients. They did not need to know how they were feeling. Both of them knew only too well. They were showing me if I only had the wit to take notice. For both of them it was a matter of dealing with internal material, deeply embedded from early experience in extremely influential interpersonal relationships, organised into highly controlling anxiety states. In both instances their family of origin proved to be the psycho-dramatic centre of their suffering.

Reflecting back to the Introduction I hope the reader will notice at this point that I have not used the term 'object relations' so far in this therapeutic discourse. But I have introduced the notion of an interpersonal relationship. For me the term 'object' (derived mainly from the work of Melanie Klein, 1932) implies something less than properly human and personal. Fortunately, the work of what is sometimes described as the middle school psychoanalysts (Fairburn, 1952; Guntripp, 1968; Winnicott, 1958) emphasises the worth, significance and continuing importance of relationships between human beings, although the terms 'object' and 'object relations' continue to be used. I have already mentioned that the term 'relational' has come to be used by some therapists to emphasise the value of the client and her special autonomy. This attracts me to that outlook and framework of reference. General practitioners of medicine need to recognise the individual response of their patients to medication, realising that although the general prescription is a guide, it is no more than a guide and highly individual responses can be expected. Such is the case, too, for us in our work with our clients. It is likely that a 'probable truism' may exist but it is also essential to remember that in the application of our techniques, reflective of these truths, we can expect highly individual responses. Then our personal response is called upon, where we may need to abandon the 'accepted' interpretation or remark and seek a fresh creative response to our client. This is sometimes more easily said than done. It usually means the therapist is taking a risk in which she might just as well fail as succeed. In this book I am attempting to imply the relational presence of value in all that I write about clients, myself and colleagues. To that end I am consciously eschewing the use of much formal abstract language that now inhabits the pages of many books on psychoanalytic psychotherapy. I am striving to be plain spoken, but please forgive me if I fail.

1 The First Encounter

The telephone rings and rings and rings. I pick it up and speak my number, very neutrally. This is often the beginning of an adventure for the person who rings and the person who is rung. In the introduction I suggested that both the client and the therapist experience very explicit fantasies, long before the first appointment is made to mutually assess one another and to enter into a psychotherapeutic relationship. This is especially true for the client for whom this is probably a novel experience.

At the beginning, the psychotherapist therapist (with only her own experience of being a client to relate to) sees that the fantasies concerning the approaching client are likely to be a product of the culture of psychoanalytic psychotherapy and her own unique experience as a trainee therapist. This is true of virtually all training courses in therapy and counselling, whether it be individual or group in character. Personal therapy is the absolute requirement for entry to training. And so the fantasies are projective. The image of the approaching client will of necessity contain many elements of the therapist herself, especially in relation to her own experience as a former client of a psychotherapist or counsellor.

At this stage there is nothing concrete to go on, but the voice on the telephone carries much implicit information. I have to deal with my own reaction of distaste when the voice is small and hesitant, male or female. Equally, I must not get carried away with enthusiasm when the voice is firm, clear and well modulated.

Although the newly arrived therapist will have known other therapists in the process of her training therapy, these relationships do not offer much in the way of a true guide of what is to come. Suddenly the client appears as a person: autonomous and separate, looking for a therapist. The therapist is in the process of being chosen, as she looks for a client. I hope these sentences point the way to a unique relationship that is about to commence. It probably needs to be said here that this internal excitement is not solely the prerogative of the psychoanalytic therapist.

As a supervisor I know that counsellors report the same feelings and that clients will sometimes bring them to therapy or counselling sessions, quite explicitly. Recently a client told me she had come to see me some fifteen years earlier, travelling a long way from her home (some 70 miles) for a one-off session. She remembered me as 'kind' and this had recently influenced her choice of me as a therapist when she discovered I was now within walking distance of her home. Between whiles she had encountered much therapy, which she experienced as punitive or 'unkind'. It varied from the female, distant, silent therapist to the rough and tumble of group analysis with a consultant psychotherapist, the latter being medically qualified. From my point of view this gave me rich material to work with. Although I shall develop the concept at greater length at a later stage of this book, it is worth noting that this notion of my 'niceness', as well as her notions of 'persecution' and 'unkindness', have to be treated cautiously. Traditional psychotherapy might suggest an immediate explanation, by virtue of the theory of transference, where the client simply interprets behaviour by the therapist as what might be described as undeserved love or hate. In other words, the therapist has supposedly done nothing to claim the love of the client any more than the hate. But in my view this is a somewhat naïve explanation of the respective positions of client and therapist. As I have become more and more experienced in clinical work, I have come to the conclusion that more often than not we as therapists do, in a certain sense, deserve the love or hate that comes our way from the client. I have always treated the idea of the opaque therapist with some suspicion, but more of that later.

Any client will have already been subject to an immense amount of overt and covert influence of a psychoanalytical character, which will have shaped and coloured her fantasies. Every day, literally every day, reference is made in the media, in private and public discussion, in newspapers, journals, in literature and films, to the thinking of Sigmund Freud and the practice of psychoanalysis. It is obvious that many contemporary psychotherapies and counselling practices are both distinctive from Freudian thought and practice and, at the same time, both consciously and unconsciously heavily influenced by Freud's tradition. None of us in Western society can avoid this influence in either its positive or negative manifestations. So the potential client, whether educated in a therapeutic milieu or not, brings this material to the decision to look for a therapist. A young woman client at her first visit glanced around my consulting room. She spotted the chaise longue and gave a little grim smile: 'You're not going to get me on that thing,' she said with a determined ring in her voice. Jacobs (1992, p. 138) confirms this view: '*It is impossible for any counsellor or therapist to ignore the influence of Freud's work, even if it has only been understood in popular form, since it is being brought daily to sessions as part of the cultural background of nearly every client.*' As a consequence, the approaching client carries an amalgam of thoughts and fancies concerning the chosen therapist. For some clients a good deal of selection activity will have taken place as these speculations impact upon deeper, more personal, material that has brought them to the therapeutic encounter. The client enters the relationship with trepidation.

The therapist waits for her client and the client looks for the therapist. There is an important difference here. The prospective client is in a proactive mode and seeks the therapist in all manner of ways. Sometimes she seeks with professional help from a doctor, a psychiatrist, social worker or psychologist, but very often this is not the case and the potential client uses a network of friends and relatives to find the therapist. She may even spot an advertisement in *Yellow Pages* or *Big Issue*. She will express attitudes concerning what she wants in the shape of a therapist. These attitudes carry the images that she has formed inside herself concerning the appearance and character of the therapist sought. It is a deeply subjective and complicated process of formation because it also calls upon conscious and unconscious memories of caring and uncaring figures from the family past and present. Anna Sands (2000) writes revealingly about her desire for a relationship with a therapist where she could behave 'like a courteous, sensible and dignified adult'. She certainly did not welcome the thought that she might regress to an infant-like state in therapy.

The *transference activity* has already begun. Earlier significant relationships will now be acted in a new, as yet not experienced, relationship.

Similarly, the therapist waits upon the coming of a client. But the therapist, although experiencing much feeling, even bodily sensations, has to wait upon the first call towards the proposed relationship. The situation is passive in that respect. I waited upon my very first client full of expectation and dread. I knew her coming would confirm for me all the work in training that I was putting into my wish to be a psychotherapist. This unknown figure would, when she arrived, lodge as an iconic figure in the process of my training as a therapist. She would symbolise the reality of my intentions, and my relationship with her would be subject to the most intimate scrutiny, through supervision, that I had ever experienced in my life beyond the intimacy, security and secrecy of my marriage. And, of course, there is the matter of money. Man must have bread to live. More of that later.

The curious factor in this matter is that although I have somewhat dramatised the situation for the trainee therapist waiting upon her first client, the sense of expectation (with its accompanying creative tension) can be expected to occur and re-occur throughout the professional lifetime of the therapist or counsellor. For the client it is much the same story. Even now when entering into personal therapy as an 'experienced' client I still feel the mounting fantasy activity within as I approach the therapist. One of the rewards of psychotherapy is this excitement in the awaited encounter – whether it comes to the client or the therapist. No matter how busy I am, and although after twenty years of practice I am much rehearsed in the experience of the approaching client, whether it be for therapy or supervision, there still occurs this lively, hopeful energy of expectation: a mixture of hope and dread. When my doorbell rings announcing the arrival of a new client I rise from my chair just that little more eagerly and, straightening my posture, I walk to answer the bell and open my door. There is a spring in my step. I am eager for the encounter.

Example

I can hardly begin to describe the fever of anticipation that occupied me as I travelled by train from the north of England to the Midlands, to join a psychotherapy group, a required part of a psychotherapy training course. I had only the slightest experience of being in that role. In a former academic career I had been a group conductor, teaching group processes and the formation of group roles, with particular attention to the characteristics of group leadership. But I had never been in an analytic group as a client/patient. All through the journey I was ruminating expectantly on what I was to encounter. I was most preoccupied with the character of the group therapist. Man or woman? I could not decide which I preferred or hoped for. I knew I had a kind of latent fear of a punitive, critical woman, whereas somewhere inside I felt I could cope with such a man. As for the rest of the group I was making certain assumptions. I guessed we would be balanced in terms of gender and age, imagining a plentiful pool of candidates for the course. I could not, try as I might, summon up pictures of them as individuals. I hoped it would not be dominated by medical personnel and that there would be some feisty group members, men as well as women. I could sense the beginning of regression in me with some pleasure. I even thought about tactics of behaviour. I weighed up the advantages of spontaneity as against deliberation. I knew the imperative would be to communicate through free association with as little censorship as possible, as advocated by Barnes, Ernst and Hyde (1999, p. 22). But I also felt a strong resistance to this command. After all, who were these people who expected me to reveal all?

This description is recalled as a very partial memory of the chaotic material zooming about inside me on that particular day. However, I'm sure that to the casual onlooker I appeared to be calmly reading a paperback book on a train. With the above description, I hope I have given some indication of the mental energy excited by the prospect of group psychotherapy, even before reaching or experiencing the group. It is important to note that all this feeling was available to me consciously but there would certainly have been activity inside me that was unconscious, exerting its influence. At that moment it would have been quite impossible for me to recognise which belonged where.

Similarly, as the client stands on the doorstep and perhaps nervously rings the doorbell, a series of internal responses operate, some of which are very evident to the client, but sometimes not. At this juncture the unconscious already holds a depth of response to this new and challenging situation, which awaits the appropriate cue to be revealed and experienced consciously by the client. However, it is quite possible that the client will only react to unconscious prompting and not become aware of the source of the behaviour. I recall one client who upon my opening the door of my house virtually fell into my arms; he was alarmed and embarrassed by this occurrence. But it provided good material for discussion. Even in this preliminary encounter the therapeutic culture spoke loud and clear and his embarrassment was quickly transformed into rather rueful and amused recognition of his feelings towards the encounter. As the therapist involved I was able to hold him momentarily and prevent him from falling, and this became a metaphor for the future of the therapy and a pointer to his deepest desire. After he recovered his balance and to some extent his composure, I watched him as he scrutinised both the physical surroundings of my entrance hall and myself. My hope was that we would pass muster. As is my custom, I showed him the therapy room and invited him to take a chair. Leaving him I said I would join him shortly, providing a moment for reflection and composure both for the client and myself before the first relational moves are made in the therapy room.

And what of the therapy room? Working in a hospital I had no control or even significant influence in the provision of an interview room or, for that matter, a therapy room. They were invariably inadequate, dingy, small and impersonal and far from secure; intrusion was possible at any time! But in my private practice I have always placed emphasis upon the therapy room as being an environment of importance (Feasey, 2000). So the furnishings, decorations and domestic objects are consciously chosen. I always remember the amusement I felt when I visited the Freud museum in Hampstead and entered the room that had been arranged to replicate Freud's consulting room in Vienna. One thing was obvious. It was not bland and discreet. It revealed a great deal about Sigmund Freud. He was not over-concerned with the issue of promoting fantasies that would impede the transference feelings of his client. I was somewhat reassured by this discovery. This presentation is sometimes in very direct contrast to the spaces provided by contemporary individual and group psychotherapists who determine to work in a minimalist environment where their personal taste, style and enthusiasms, unlike Freud's, are not evident.

Another concern I have addressed in private practice is to provide private, secure accommodation and reasonable comfort both for my clients and myself. My aim is to place the client and myself on an equal social level, as far as is possible in the circumstances. A further desire is to place psychotherapy firmly in the region of domesticity, removed from a clinical setting. So what is called for is evidence of domestic life: there is good carpet, solid comfortable chairs, against the wall is a chaise longue (a gesture towards analysis), one or two framed photos of scenes of family life, and the walls are decorated in soft creamy tones. Some quiet, decorative abstract artworks are on the walls. The lighting is indirect, good quality curtains hang at the window. All this furnishing and decoration is food for fantasy and speculation for the entering client. Much of it will be absorbed unconsciously. It is likely that for most of my clients the decorations will simply produce a general effect of comfort, security and privacy. I imagine for others it might seem 'posh', bourgeois and unwanted. As the therapist I am very familiar with this scene, although it only takes a small disturbance either inside or outside of me to alert me to its properties.

Example

Judith referred herself to me by telephone. I received the call and briefly spoke with the caller to make an appointment. I thought I was speaking to Judith, but I was wrong. Judith was profoundly deaf and her sister made the original appointment. When Judith entered my hallway I was not aware of her deafness. She smiled briefly. I pointed to the therapy room and invited her to enter. My usual gesture. I said I would join her shortly and asked her to make herself comfortable, merely pointing out where I would sit. When I returned a few minutes later I was shocked. The wall light had been turned off. Although my chair had not been touched, the client's chair had been brought up in close proximity to a degree I had never before experienced. I went to my seat and looked closely at Judith. She sensed my discomfort and perhaps my somewhat fearful irritation. She quickly explained herself: 'I am profoundly deaf. I need to have the top light on and the light behind your head off so that I can lip read you. OK?' I leaned back in my chair mollified. 'Oh, and I must be close too.' She smiled. This gave me an opening. 'Well, we almost certainly will get close as time goes on. I see you don't waste anytime getting things arranged your way.'

It was obvious she understood everything I said and I noted that her voice tone betrayed no sign of her deafness. I was aware through self supervision that my anxiety level had dropped and I was able to see her more clearly, the mist of defensive feeling in me had cleared.

Although I maintained composure during this interaction I had in fact felt an immediate sense of loss of control with accompanying anxiety as I entered the room and sat down. I noticed that Judith too appeared to watch me closely looking for a reaction. I think my verbal response, reaffirming the nature of our relationship, helped both Judith and myself. There was much to follow in the ensuing therapeutic work concerning issues of control and emotional abuse.

Once this initial encounter had passed and we had settled into mutual appraisal I realised I liked the look of my client. She had a slightly exotic look. Dark hair and eyes and long flashing fingers spoke of a degree of freedom and personal assertion that I found immediately attractive. On the other hand, her intense look was somewhat disconcerting and, although I rationalised her need to watch my lips closely, I still found the scrutiny disconcerting. What also came to me, but quite how I do not know, was her interest in the proposed therapy and a determination to work hard at achieving a good result for herself.

How did I know all this within a few moments of meeting my client? I do not know and neither does any one else. Indeed the subtleties of both conscious and unconscious communication are beyond any but the crudest understanding. But we are all aware how quickly first impressions are recorded and held and acted upon, sometimes appropriately, sometimes not. I was aware all the time of my reactions to this new client but I could only guess at her reactions to me. On the surface there appeared to be a cheerful challenging pose. I knew that I would have to watch my step, be prepared to justify any observations or interpretations I might make. And so it proved to be as the negotiations opened up between us in establishing the therapeutic contract. I was aware too of a degree of suspicion in the air of our conversation. It appeared to be linked with what I perceived as her disability. I had worked before with people with a disability but never with a deaf person. What became clear very soon was that my notion of my client's perceived disability was accompanied by a whole range of assumptions that were more a product of my own deficiencies then anything else. Here was a woman who saw herself as whole, not deficient; furthermore she was a champion of deaf people. These were issues that would emerge forcefully over time but I sensed their presence in the first confused moments of the encounter, and I believe she did too.

So here is the complexity, only partially described, of the material of a first encounter. Each time we meet a new client this process takes place, and each engagement is new and original, promoting highly specific responses in us that have to be acknowledged and dealt with as best as we can.

It is relatively easy for me to give an account of this first encounter from my own memories of them taking place. It is much more difficult to recount the experience of the client at this critical meeting but I am firmly of the opinion that as we start so we go on. That is not to say that the *early transference feelings* (Freud and Breuer, 1895) that operate in the beginning of the relationship are never modified. I am sure they are and often the therapeutic progress of the client can be identified through the subtle changes experienced in the therapeutic relationship. Indeed, it is a major aim in therapy that these shifts take place as powerful elements of change for the client. Having said that, it also never ceases to amaze me how the feelings of the first encounter continue to manifest throughout the course of therapy.

Throughout this chapter I have been exploring the nature of the first encounter. As client and therapist we are assessing each other. For the most part the client assesses us informally – she responds to the therapeutic dialogue and gets a sense of the nature of the therapist and the therapist's stance. She receives powerful sensory impressions of our presence. In my case I am over seventy years old. This will make an impact, especially where the client herself is much younger, as is usually the case. She either responds warmly or not in this interview and, as a result, will take what is usually a quick decision, to stay or go. The therapist, however, is in a more formal situation during this assessment time. Depending upon her orientation and training a number of assessment procedures will be followed. I do not intend to outline them in all their variety here. No matter how intellectually systematic we may be as therapists in the assessment procedure we are still powerfully guided by our feelings. Although we do not yet have a league table of patient responses to be represented as numbers from one to ten, nevertheless there are pressures in the field of psychotherapy seeking to influence us in our judgement of our clients when we first encounter them. I have been somewhat alarmed to come across psychoanalytic literature, in particular, that attempts to signify features of patient assessment indicating whether the subject is a 'suitable case for treatment', to coin an old and intimidating phrase (Feasey, 2000, pp. 42–5). Whatever the approach, it is quite certain that deeply subjective factors play upon the assessment meeting influencing both client and therapist. I can well recall a young colleague coming out of an assessment meeting for individual psychotherapy, in a hospital setting, breathing rather deeply and complaining loudly about the attitude of the intended patient. She concluded her remarks with an abrupt dismissal: 'Anyway, he was totally concrete, no sign of insight or psychological curiosity in his thinking.' I looked out of the office window and saw the figure of an overweight, poorly dressed, fifty-year-old man walking rather disconsolately away from the psychotherapy unit. He was about my age and shape. I murmured: 'Perhaps he ought to seek a second opinion.' My colleague grinned at me: 'You would say that!'

I have noticed that clients seeking therapy in private practice are often quite willing to shop around for a therapist who they feel will suit them. The NHS does not encourage such behaviour and most psychotherapy units probably interpret such behaviour as pathological. It is common to hear rather dramatic language employed to account for a patient's dissatisfaction. She may be dismissed as having 'insatiable needs' or 'being deeply embedded in primitive states of hatred and rejection, of having not fully emerged from the depressive or paranoid schizoid position'. Sometimes I think Melanie Klein has much to answer for!

On the other hand it has disconcerted me when I realise that I am merely one of perhaps three different therapists being assessed as suitable by a potential client. This happened recently.

The circumstances were quite interesting. The woman came to see me having apparently found my name in the UKCP (United Kingdom Council for Psychotherapy) register. She was looking for psychoanalytic therapy. I was prepared for her arrival and had taken some trouble at preparing some further referral information if our discussion did not result in a contract of therapy. She was an experienced client moving into my town from another part of the country. At the end of an hour I concluded the interview and asked if she wanted to pay me 'now' or should I send an invoice in relation to our session together. She looked taken aback and made no firm commitment either way leaving my room quite quickly. I waited about three weeks for a response from her, wondering if she had found another therapist or would return. Then I wrote a short letter asking about her intentions and enclosing my usual invoice for £20. She was, I might add, a well-paid professional person. I quickly received an email refusing to pay my fee and stating she assumed that it was normal practice for an 'advisory' interview to be free. I replied that this was not my experience. I decided to waive the fee, but not without some feelings of hurt and resentment. In retrospect, I think my so-called waiver was merely face-saving, as I subconsciously knew that she had no intention of paying me.

Another feature of assessment interviews is the recording of the interview, sometimes described as taking a history. Is there truly any point in doing this? I would at one time write a long account of these early meetings, partly as history-taking, partly recording my thoughts and feelings towards the client or patient. In this respect I was emulating a consultant I worked with, for whom I had great respect. In addition, I was following customary hospital practice where 'notes' follow the patient wherever she may go and are regarded as sacrosanct. Sometimes a well-meaning nurse would bring a patient to my interview room, handing over a bulky set of notes at the same time. I would invariably politely refuse them, saying I could quite easily manage an interview without the notes.

My reason for not wishing to take the notes was quite simple. I did not wish to impede the flow of conversation between the patient and myself by rifling through the notes. On the contrary, I wanted the encounter to be a fresh experience for myself and I wanted the patient to experience meeting me in the same kind of way. It seems quite obvious that psychotherapy being an encounter embedded in the relationship of client and therapist must hold onto this intimate and neo-conversational character. It has to be acknowledged that the conversation is going to be radically different from the simple exchanges and pleasantries with friends, colleagues, neighbours and relatives, but nevertheless the meeting benefits from a conversational atmosphere. Scribbling away at length on a clipboard throughout the interview does not assist the process. I suppose the reading of case notes after the interview may prove to be useful and illuminating especially when it appears the patient has been highly resistant to psychiatric intervention, refusing drugs or failing to maintain the appropriate regime. Sometimes the reports of behaviour on a ward, which are frequently judgemental and moralistic, make controversial reading, especially following a psychotherapy interview where the patient has recognised and responded to a therapeutic relationship offered by the therapist.

Example

I received a call in the hospital office, where I worked sessionally for some years. The caller, a woman consultant, wanted me to do a psychotherapy assessment with a young woman, Gill, who was currently on a 'closed forensic ward'. An uncle had sexually abused this young woman for many years, from childhood to adolescence. He would bring her into his sitting room in his bachelor flat and play pornographic videos on his TV set, whilst at the same time fondling her breasts and vagina. The end would come when he would open his trousers and she would have to masturbate him to orgasm. At the age of seventeen she rebelled and sitting beside him on a sofa, when he opened his trousers and displayed his penis, she produced a knife and struck him a blow in the stomach. She called for an ambulance, but he died a miserable and distressing death. Technically she was a murderess. She had, however, been found 'unfit to plead', which had resulted in her incarceration in the mental hospital. The consultant told me the story and I rang the ward to arrange an interview. The following Thursday I went along to the ward and rang the admission bell. I was greeted by cheerful male nurse who was expecting me. The first problem arose. He wanted me to be chap-eroned throughout the interview. I pointed out that this was inappropriate and unnecessary. I did not feel either Gill or I were likely to be in any danger during the interview. After a struggle I got my own way through a compromise. The interview room door would be left open so we could be observed. I conducted the interview for an hour and after this I felt that another meet-ing would be helpful to both of us, and Gill agreed. She was eager to talk and it felt therapeutic being with her. I pointed out I could not come for another week because I was a part-time ther-apist. Gill accepted this with what appeared to be good grace. Before leaving the ward I spoke to the male ward nurse and he appeared to be reassured at the outcome of the assessment inter-view. However, his last words as I left were 'Don't forget she's a murderer!'

The next time I came to the ward I was told she had been moved to another city to a more secure regime because she was violent. It transpired that she had become distressed on the ward. The nursing staff and a junior doctor tried to tranquillise her with a hypodermic injection, and the doctor had been hit across the face in the course of the fracas.

I spoke to the consultant and she said that regretfully nothing could be done and there was no psychotherapeutic presence at the secure unit the girl had gone to.

So the label 'murderer' had triumphed and my psychothera-peutic intervention was discounted.

My practice as far as written records are concerned is simply to note facts that need to be recorded to ensure a continuity of communication. That and little else.

Before concluding this chapter a reference must be made to the practice of making a formulation following the assessment interviews. Today it is regarded as an imperative for trainee ther-apists to make a formulation following a number of in-depth interviews. This formulation calls upon the trainee's knowledge of psychoanalytic theory to construct a clinical picture of the client. This surely derives from the medical influence that has been apparent in psychotherapy and psychoanalysis for many years. I realise I sound sceptical about the use of this. If psychotherapy is to have any distinction at all it rests upon the realisation that it works when it proceeds through a relationship which, although firm and dependable in structure, is also tentative and exploratory in its process. To start the relationship with a formulation, where the therapist explains to herself (after a few interviews) the definitive origins and construct of the client's difficulties, seems to be putting the horse before the cart. Nevertheless it is very popular in certain psychotherapy centres and training organisations, especially those dominated by a medical or academic culture. I would suggest that if a formulation comes quickly to mind in the early interviews then it should be put aside and treated with caution. The most that usually appears in early assessment interviews is a surface presentation of anxiety and distress that has brought the client to seek therapy. This will usually trigger speculation in the therapist, but it should be remembered that this is only speculation and needs to be treated with caution. Often, too, the client is testing out the therapist to see what kind of attention is being given to what is being presented, and how serious it is thought to be. The genuineness of the therapist is being tested and therefore the more trusting the response by the therapist the more likelihood there is of a mutually satisfying contract for therapy. Any preconceived idea can only impede this process.

2 Feelings: Transference, Counter-Transference, Gut Feeling and Sex

Transference

> It is my view that healing takes place in a situation of intimacy around a vulnerable and damaged area and that, in order to have access to that area, the therapist must conduct himself as an ordinary and decent human being. He must have the capacity to 'be there'.
>
> (Ashley, 2003)

> The concept of transference turns on the fact that we don't meet other people as much as we construct them, based on experiences going back to childhood. The same therapist will be experienced by one patient as a forbidding father and by another as a compassionate mother.
>
> (Luepnitz, 2003)

I feel as one with Jill Ashley when she states what seems to me to be a first condition of psychotherapy – hence the sub-title of this book. But, and this is a big 'but', the situation between client and therapist is both more and less than is implied by the statement I quote above. The 'but' is suggested by the quote from Ann Deborah Luepnitz (2003) above.

In Chapter 1, I insisted upon a recognition of feelings that arise in the first and early encounters between therapist and client before each has had enough time to process the feelings, placing them firmly and safely into the relationship. Safety of feelings, in this situation, seems to rest upon the conscious recognition of the feelings that are being felt in the therapeutic relationship in its opening encounters. Then the feelings are put on hold until enough time and attention has been given to them to ensure the usefulness of their presence in the therapy. That this happens in the therapeutic relationship is well known and recognised by practising therapists and their clients, especially when the latter reflect upon their first encounters and the feelings that then arose in them. Sometimes this came as a surprise to them, and sometimes as something of a shock. I will not burden the reader with the endless references that can be found to the phenomenon of transference that can be found in contemporary psychoanalytic and psychodynamic literature. I will simply take the reader back to Freud's own words on the subject. Ronald W. Clark (1982, p. 104) reports a dramatic letter that Freud wrote to Stefan Zweig:

> On the evening of the day when all her symptoms had been disposed of, he [Breuer] was summoned to the patient again and found her confused and writhing in abdominal cramps. Asked what was wrong with her, she replied: 'Now Dr Breuer's child is coming.'

Failing to recognise and understand the nature of this event Breuer literally panicked, withdrew from the patient, and handed her to a colleague. He then promptly went on holiday with his wife. Given the state he was in this was probably the best thing to do. This is possibly the earliest reportage of what has come to be known as *transference feelings* in the psychotherapeutic relationship. It has, of course, been placed in the possession of psychoanalysis, but in reality it is a common phenomenon and occurs spontaneously in many social situations, especially where figures are likely to be idealised or denigrated. However, Breuer was not the only person to be thrown into confusion by the seductive activity by a patient. Jung in a letter to Freud reported on a female patient:

> She was, so to speak, my test case, for which reason I remembered her with special gratitude and affection. Since I knew from experience that she would immediately relapse if I withdrew my support, I prolonged the relationship over the years and in the end found myself morally obliged, as it were, to devote a large measure of friendship to her, until I saw that an unintended wheel had started turning, where upon I broke with her. She was of course systematically planning my seduction, which I considered inopportune. Now she is seeking revenge. . . .
>
> (quoted in McGuire & McGlashan, 1974, p. 150)

Jung goes on to describe the rumours the patient had spread about him, all of a sexual character, which he felt undermined his professional position. Freud replied: 'I myself have never been taken in so badly, but I have come very close to it a number of times, and had a narrow escape.' These are somewhat dramatic accounts of the occurrence of erotic love being found in the therapeutic relationship which, as far as we know, were unintended by the male therapist. Most psychoanalytic psychotherapists are familiar with this kind of material and sometimes report similar experiences arising from their own practice. Often the suggestion is that the eroticism had been unprovoked. Frankly, I am sceptical of these claims. It is noticeable in the instances quoted from Jung and Freud's experience that they both feel that they had somehow brought it upon themselves. In Jung's case it is obvious. Freud is less revealing but his 'narrow escape' phrase suggests that he, too, somehow got close to what could have been a compromising situation with a female patient. There is often an assumption that well-trained therapists are secure and protected in their professional skill, and even when erotic material emerges, and attaches itself to them, they are impervious to its influence. I would certainly accept that the training aims towards the protection of patient and therapist alike in this respect, but human beings being human will sometimes err in respect of erotic proposals, with pretty unhappy consequences. I have been impressed recently by Susie Orbach's (1999) frank discussion of the many feelings that have been stirred up in her in early encounters with clients, even to the extent that she has felt disturbing and puzzling physical reactions. More recently in an article in the *British Journal for Psychotherapy* she speculates about the body and its appearance. She writes:

> Let's go a step further. How does the way in which I am in my body affect your feelings about your body? Does it make you more or less self aware? Does my body presence sanction, confirm, disturb, turn you off, overwhelm you? Does it please you? What does it tell you about you and your body and your relation to other bodies?   (Orbach, 2003)

Oddly enough I was immediately reminded of the only occasion I actually saw Susie Orbach speak, some fifteen years ago. She came to a meeting held in the local theatre studio in the town where I then lived with my wife and family. My wife came as well, and we were conscious that the meeting was portrayed as a women's issue event and there would be present a number of local feminists. I felt the meeting would be intensely political and that attracted me. And yet now, all these years later, I cannot remember a thing of which she spoke. However, I do remember clearly the discomfort of the meeting very well. Susie Orbach came onto the centre of the spotlit stage, and the first thing I noticed was that she was wearing a rather tight dress. She sat down and grinned at us in a friendly manner, and then quite unconsciously (I think) she began to pick at the edge of her dress, as if pulling it down to cover more of her legs. She appeared to squirm a little. I felt uncomfortable and mirrored her squirm. And so it went on and on through the meeting. At the end of the evening, while walking home with my wife, I drew attention to my experience. She confirmed my feelings and then burst into laughter and song: 'Well it's my body and I'll squirm if I want too!'

Orbach's 2003 article took me back all those years and I am happy to confirm her suggestions. Certainly her body did make me aware, most uncomfortably, of my own body. She left what is called a 'lasting impression' as if I had been imprinted with her discomfort, or at least what I took to be her discomfort. And so there I was in the grip of a counter-transference. I am not sure it mattered very much: after all, although I was then a new inexperienced psychotherapist, she was not my client.

There is another factor here which I have not seen addressed by Susie Orbach and that is the issue of her being a 'known' personality. She appears on television, gives her views on the radio and writes popular therapeutic journalism as well as professional articles. So when she is encountered 'in person' the complexity of the experience is profound, and I would expect disturbances of both a physical and emotional nature if such an event happened to me or, for that matter, any one else. It is difficult today in the current media climate not to have at least a passing 'knowledge' of her. As Freud became a 'known' figure the same issues must have arisen for him and his patients. Many years ago I had a part-time job as a television presenter with the BBC and I gave it up in part because I did not want to deal with the issues that would inevitably arise when clients saw me on the TV screen.

In a case fragment Susie Orbach even fantasises about what it would be like to have an affair with a male client, and I think this is a common experience in the counter-transference relationship.

Example

Jane was an established client. We worked together well and with a degree of openness and intimacy that made for a thoroughly satisfying therapeutic exchange in our sessions. She was a strong young woman, a health service professional working in a psychotherapy milieu, one of those who I would call the 'white coat brigade'. One day at the conclusion of a session I rose quickly from my chair to get my appointment book to confirm our next meeting. It was at this juncture that I was accustomed to receiving fees. It is my practice to work in a cash economy. As I rose to my feet and left the room I sensed a response from Jane. When I returned and sat down she smiled at me in what I could only describe as a conspiratorial way and said: 'What energy! Where do you get your energy from?' A rhetorical question of some force. And then she burst out nervously laughing. This put me into something of a dilemma. The session was over. I had another client in ten minutes. What did this mean? It was true I felt the energy in her presence and I had behaved energetically. Had my body language spoken loudly and revealed that which I was only dimly conscious of? Jane was attracted to the energy inside herself, and she apparently found it in me too. I reflected upon the situation and examined, as closely as I could, my feelings towards her but, although admiring her and feeling affectionate towards her, acknowledging her courage and willingness to work therapeutically, I did not want her sexually. I remembered suddenly, in my confusion, that she had worked in a sexually charged atmosphere where a senior therapist had emotionally abused and seduced younger, inexperienced colleagues. He was notorious for his sexual seduction of junior psychotherapy trainees, but was protected from exposure by those in authority around him. He was finally unmasked by a patient's husband who realised that this therapist was exploiting his wife for personal sexual gratification. Was there a connection? I believe there was.

Susie Orbach's (1999) very powerful description of her bodily reactions to clients resonate with me now as I write this account. My energy, the quickness as I moved about following a strong session, spoke of erotic stimulus. It must be acknowledged too that as a man in his sixties I found the admiring remark of a young woman flattering; for a moment I was seduced. (As I use this word 'seduced' I feel an intellectual restraint – I am not seduced by the implied sexual interest of the young woman but rather by my own need for reassurance in the face of diminishing physical potential, a common enough feeling as males grow older.) This feeling contrasted strongly with other occasions with clients, when I have had to drag myself from my chair feeling time worn and exhausted.

Obviously these are somewhat special moments that are being recalled. They are actually the most blatant and obvious examples of general experiences that are sometimes not at all obvious to us as therapists. Most of the time I believe we regard our performance in the therapy room as being pretty consistent in style and value, but the truth is that there is probably a good degree of variation, which we can recall, if we wish, in supervision. This variation is, I feel sure, connected with the degree of fatigue or energy that is generated in us within the therapeutic relationship. We are taught as therapists to work within the transference. This at first seems a reasonable injunction but in reality the different felt responses to transference in the relationship coming from either client or therapist can make the task very difficult.

Example

In September 2001, a horrendous criminal act of public terrorism was carried out in New York. Immediately following it every client coming to me for therapy wanted to talk about the event. What was to be my response? I felt that to 'interpret' their anger and anxiety as merely neurotic aspects of the personality or making connections with their own life history may be inappropriate. However, as they spoke my own memories returned, of being in my bed as a 13-year old whilst bombs fell, explosions rattled the air and the familiar broken drone of German bombers was heard overhead. I felt fear then and it came back to my memory as the clients spoke to me. The clients had realistic fears to express, moral outrage to express and political judgements to be given expression in our therapy session. I, too, was full of feeling, most of it sadness in response to what had taken place and fear for the likely outcome. Obviously transference issues are awakened in this example. Would it have been appropriate to raise issues of transference in this moment? I am sure my clients assumed me to be a sympathetic listener who probably shared their viewpoints. Indeed for the most part I did. One of the clients took up a critical position towards the policies of the UK and USA governments and stated them forcefully; it did not seem to occur to him that I might not share his point of view; indeed he assumed I shared his anger. I felt it would not have been at all appropriate to raise transference issues with him at this moment in our relationship. And in any case I heartily agreed with his conclusions. The best I could do was to allow, without intervention or interpretation, the genuine feelings of these clients within the context of a major international political, social and moral event.

The difficulty and the task in the therapy room is to sort out what might be called issues of reality from those that are vested in fantasy, and this is not always clear cut. When external events bear down heavily upon the therapeutic relationship we need to consider the question of transference carefully. I am not of the school (*mostly* Kleinian, 1975) that believes that all transactions in the therapy room are of a transference character – to believe so seems to me to disturb and distort the meaning and significance of transference as described by Freud and Breuer (1974). I stay with the idea that transference feelings in the therapy room are the result of a number of psychological transactions between the therapist and the client. The powerful feelings that clients experience, inside themselves, may be the result of a false connection with the therapist, whereby a relationship is imagined and believed in, but which is not supported by the actual social and emotional behaviour of the therapist. This is a normal and expected emotional response by a client to the unique relationship offered by the therapist. Early psychoanalysts were surprised that their clients appeared to 'fall in love' with them and it certainly alarmed some of them. But time and good therapy work soon exposed the fallacious nature of these feelings and gradually, as therapy continued, a more realistic response from the client to the therapist was observed. Obviously, the response of a therapist may be inappropriate when a client appears to wish to eroticise a relationship, and in recent years there has been a growing literature of books and articles describing sexual abuse in the therapy relationship. It has to be acknowledged, too, that sometimes the client falls into a hate rather than a love relationship towards the therapist, and in this case the therapist has to be just as careful in his response. Indeed, I regard this as the more dangerous situation. The fact that the therapist is not being seduced or invited into a sexual relationship allows 'hate' easier then 'love'. Sometimes a therapist may mistakenly believe his own 'hate' for the client to be justified. But it is very rare indeed for such a justification to be supported by the reality of the situation, any more than undeserved 'love' can be.

As mentioned above, some psychoanalytic schools now suggest that all emotional transactions in the therapy room are transferential exchanges. It can be argued that this is so but it is also obvious to the experienced practising therapist that the level, intensity and quality of emotional activity in the therapy room varies a great deal from one meeting to another, and from one client to another. There is a need to discriminate in therapeutic judgement as these transactions take place. The other important aspect of transference is that sometimes the feelings projected towards the therapist, and imagined as belonging to the client–therapist relationship, derive from a relationship experienced elsewhere at a different time in a different context. The feelings concerned more often than not come from early childhood experiences and are often the result of *idealised memories* of, *or desires for*, parental loving care in its absence.

Example

Michelle, a young mature French woman with professional qualifications in health care, married with two young children, came for therapy complaining of intense anxiety, exhaustion and moments of deep depression that would come in waves of self-destructive ennui. She remained in therapy for two and a half years and during that time her husband left her for another woman, her work flourished, and after a period of despair and grieving for the lost marriage, her children settled into a shared caring regime. In the first year at Christmas time Michelle presented me with an expensive Christmas gift. At the moment of giving she looked at me very fondly and said, 'You are the very best of psychotherapists, a super person.' All said with a somewhat attractive French accent. For a moment I was confused and flattered. The session was ending; the therapeutic frame was melting away as the clock ticked on. I gave her a smile, thanked her and tentatively wished her a happy holiday. Then she was gone. We were due to meet again in the New Year. I weighed up the possibilities of this gift. The gift (a plant in a beautiful earthenware pot) although quite expensive was not altogether inappropriate. What was missing, of course, was the fact that on that day I had not given her a gift; on the contrary I had accepted my usual fee. These confusions are bound to enter the therapy room from time to time. As she went I gradually thought my way through the muzz of my surprised feelings and decided to present the incident in the New Year, at our next session, as a discussion of the meaning of my relationship with her and her feelings towards me.

It is obvious that this client quite reasonably felt that the relationship with me was beneficial to her and I knew she respected and enjoyed the rather conservative nature of the therapeutic regime. Nevertheless I felt this present giving, both in its form and speech, was suggesting a depth of attachment that probably sprang from transference feelings derived from an earlier emotional relationship (probably with her father). Having lost her husband (in some ways her father's successor), she was discovering feelings towards me that appeared to replicate her former unfulfilled emotional needs and satisfactions. But sometimes we need to be wary of appearances and I knew that the work we were doing together required a certain degree of disillusionment on her part. I proceeded to draw attention to her lost relationships both with her father and former husband, the limits of her relationship with me, and the question of how best to discover new ones. It was fairly obvious that she would not be free to discover and embrace a loving heterosexual relationship with another man until her hatred for the deserting husband had abated and her 'love' for me had reached a more mundane plateau of beneficence and realism.

Sometimes transference exchanges similar to this are quite obvious, but sometimes they are not and only become evident in a period of especially intense therapy where feelings well up and come to the consciousness of the client and the therapist. They can sometimes take the colour of dislike, persecution and betrayal, all powerful negatives. The issue of feelings between therapist and client is a continuing theme in psychotherapy, and it should be remembered that the therapist too can experience strong feelings towards a client that are not substantiated by any realistic emotional or social encounter. We call this 'counter-transference' but it quite clearly is of the same stuff as is experienced by the client, and it needs to be addressed by the therapist with the same professional concern. We invite our clients to address the issue of transference and, by the same token, we also should not neglect this task. Simply to acknowledge the feeling is not good enough: we need to know what brings it into our consciousness and then what we are to do with it.

Counter-Transference

Example

> Some little while ago I found myself angry and dismissive (in hate) of a woman client. She was a strong woman, strong in the sense of being able and willing to express her feelings in a powerful and meaningful way. I admired this quality in her but ironically I found its presence, when it applied to her relationship with me rather than other persons in her life, difficult to work with. I just felt angry at what I saw as an ungrateful client giving me a hard time for no apparent or at least justifiable reason. She also played around with boundaries and communication regarding appointments. The latter especially affected me and I would grumble furiously to myself about her wayward behaviour, as I saw it. I knew this anger was a problem. I began to look into myself and question its presence. It was definitely located in my

experience and feeling towards women and went back a long way.

Eventually I realised that her behaviour raised issues in me of control and helplessness in the face of a powerful female presence. I traced this back many years to a childhood beset with serious illness and certain aspects of nursing care. One aspect came from my mother who was indulgent and emotional in her response to my sickliness whilst at the same time not withholding or containing her deep anxiety each time I became ill. This was confusing. To complicate matters further I had periods of in-patient hospital treatment back in the days when parents of ill children were treated by the hospital as a nuisance. It was made clear to mothers that they abrogated their parental rights the moment their child entered the hospital ward. And so I fell into the hands of nurses, exclusively women, who were quite inconsistent in their treatment of me. Some of the junior staff were friendly and caring, in an open expressive way, but the majority of older nursing staff were bossy, cool or even cold in their management of me, especially in their handling of intimate post-operative procedures that I dreaded. These women frightened me. I found the whole atmosphere of the wards intimidating and oppressive. Later in life I was to convert this fear into anger. Some of the anger was felt towards my mother simply because as a child I did not understand why she gave me into the hands of uncaring strangers. Her own anxiety when we entered the hospital for my admission was palpable and this too frightened me and at a later time I felt very angry towards her for failing to 'stick up' for me or herself. Most of these issues I have explored and largely come to terms with. I came to realise the helplessness of my working-class mother when faced with the social and emotional force of middle-class doctors and nurses, many of whom assumed superiority over her, in an intensely hierarchical situation. I eventually began to understand the medical culture that so forcefully held doctors and nurses in its sway and from this began the process of forgiving these ancient historical punitive iconic figures inhabiting my mind and imagination.

My unloving and critical client, apparently dismissive of any feelings I might have, dismissive of my carefully constructed routines and boundaries, was treading on dangerous ground – dangerous for me and for her and I had to tread carefully and, as Casement (1985) points out, with a high degree of self-aware-ness in my internal supervision, which I applied to working with this client.

These feelings are technically referred to as counter-transfer-ence. Here the meaning is not limited to feelings being directed against the client. 'Counter' in this context simply means moving towards the client, away from the self, arising from the relation-ship with the client in the therapeutic situation but the material coming from other experience belonging to the therapist, outside the relationship. The example I give above of my 'hatred' of my unloving client demonstrates how powerful and unreasonable this experience might prove to be. In this instance it was hate but obviously it could just as easily have been love. I use the words 'hate' and 'love', knowing that they are loaded with meaning. I intend them to be read and understood as terms that encompass, in each instance, the full range of possible feelings that can be identified as deriving from these terms. So, for example, quite strong irritation with a client would be encompassed by the term 'hate' in the context of therapy, whereas feelings of approval towards a client would fall into the category of 'love'.

Dinora Pines (1993) writes with illumination on this topic and ends a chapter on the subject rather ruefully in the following manner:

> my own analytic experience has lead me to believe that the careful monitoring of the infinite variety of transference and counter transference phenomena that are revealed in the course of analysis are among the most creative and exciting aspects of our work. Yet at the same time these phenomena remain some of the most intriguing, bewildering and confus-ing aspects of our therapeutic endeavour; they engage the analyst in constant re-examination of her own internal world as well as that of the patient. And I shall leave you with the question that a patient put to me the other day: 'Is transfer-ence love real love?' I hope you will find the answer.

I hope so too.

Gut Feeling

But what of 'gut feeling'? People will state, as if it is definitive evidence, that when encountering a relationship or social experience for the first time they had a 'gut feeling' about the encounter, to which they paid special attention. This phrase is often used to explain or justify an ensuing judgement. The 'gut feeling' can be positive or negative. Is this feeling different from what we understand as transference? I am not sure, but the one feature that seems to give it a significance of its own is the 'gut feeling' felt almost immediately upon meeting a stranger. Although all of us have enough social poise not to reveal our 'gut feeling', we are always aware of its presence in an encounter. Perhaps the unconscious is activated by a special response to an unknown perceptual signal that connects with an earlier experience in which strong feelings of attraction or repulsion were felt. We can only understand so much of the internal world and when it is revealed in this way it should excite curiosity in us as therapists. Most people would recognise that the 'gut feeling' frequently has a sexual component to it. This is not the same as the feelings of romantic love described by poets and songwriters, nor is it the same as feelings of opportunistic lust. It is as if something deeper and more serious, in emotional terms, has been activated. The 'gut feeling' as a slang term describes something deep inside us not readily accessible to rationality, literally in the stomach (and the stomach is often, in popular parlance, felt as a place of intense emotional response, for instance in the expression 'I felt my stomach turn over').

Example

Jeremy stood on the doorstep. His face held in a mask of suspicious control was tight, narrow and grey. He looked hungry. He looked cold. He looked angry. To my surprise in this moment of encounter on the doorstep, in the brief moment before I invited him into the house I felt a wave of warmth and sympathy (love) well up in me. It felt very physical. I suppressed a big smile and an enthusiastic welcome. That would have been quite inappropriate in this first meeting, in this first encounter of minuscule time.

He stepped into the hall passing me, going towards the therapy room door, which I gestured towards, inviting him to go in, to make himself comfortable. His face betrayed no feeling other than reserve, distance, with a hint of suspicion. I left him for a few minutes and then returned to the room. He was sitting in an armchair, his body held upright, a little tense, he stared at me through his 'granny glasses', National Health with the plastic removed from the rims. We scrutinised each other. He was waiting for me to speak. I waited for him. A moment passed and I decided to break the silence. I welcomed him, told him I would make a few notes but after today there would be no more note-taking in the therapy sessions and then I asked him to tell me why he had come. Another sustained silence held us apart. Then quite unexpectedly he started into a harsh condemnation of a clinical psychology department in the south of England where he had sought help the year before. He ended a diatribe with the words 'I was sick of them, sick, sick of them, the shits!'

A response came to me immediately: 'And it's pouring out of you both ends. That must be a relief.' He gave me a great grin and laughed a sour laugh.

I felt my gut feeling for him as he entered the house was justified and I knew I could relax and work with him. All this occurred in a few moments, which floods into our being so quickly that analysis is very difficult. Thinking about it afterwards I came to a tentative conclusion. Maybe I was finding in him an earlier version of aspects of myself when I was younger, certainly younger than he was then. My tentative conclusion was the result of intellectual speculation but my feelings and words in the session had not been thought through. I had behaved spontaneously and I trusted my response on that moment. I continued to keep a very close eye on my feelings for him and as things turned out I was justified in my trust in myself. We worked together productively for a couple of years and parted with mutual feelings of satisfaction.

Sex

Freud was openly attacked and derided for his conclusion that female hysteria, as he then understood it, was the result of sexual trauma. He saw desire, guilt and anxiety occurring in childhood, working its way through to the sexual unfolding of adolescence, when it failed to be resolved in a satisfactory emotional sexual experience, the earlier sexual experience, in its morbidity, serving in adolescence to inhibit and distort a proper sexual maturation. Even today many psychoanalysts have turned away from Freud's early conclusions and it is possible to read many case studies in psychoanalytic journals that barely mention the presence of early sexual experience in the life of patients. In recent years, as an all-encompassing world of child sexual abuse has come to light, there has been angry reaction to the neglect by therapists (of virtually all schools) of the significance of early pathological sexual experience. The victims in particular have spoken out loudly and have at last been taken notice of. The point of these observations is to draw attention to the obvious which is all too often ignored, namely that both men and women spend a lifetime experiencing their gender as perhaps the most critical defining feature of existence. With it goes the experience of sexual feelings colouring and shaping virtually all their relationships both within their gender and between the genders. It is a banal truism that men spend a disproportionate part of every day experiencing and reflecting upon their sexual response to other men and women. I am somewhat bleakly amused that this is rarely said of women – a clear example of censorship and repression. For centuries it has been dangerous to admit the intense sexuality of women, other than through religious inhibition that can place an undue stress upon it as threatening and dangerous. In my view it is no different for the psychotherapists and counsellors with whom I have worked, and I am encouraged when my supervisees, both men and women, report their sexual feelings in the supervision session.

It is accepted as a first principle by most training courses that sex between therapist and client is a matter of serious disciplinary concern. The novel *Disgrace* by J. M. Coetzee captures instant attention when the central protagonist in the book, a middle-aged professor of English literature, admits to a disciplinary enquiry to having sexual intercourse with a young woman student. He states:

I was walking through the old college gardens and, so it happened, was the young woman in question, Ms Isaacs. Our paths crossed. Words passed between us, and at that moment something happened which, not being a poet, I will not try to describe. Suffice it to say that Eros entered. After that I was not the same.

This statement confuses and outrages some members of the committee of enquiry, especially the women members – one of whom particularly loathes his action. This is to be his downfall, such is the power of what is perceived as a sexual misdemeanour in Western society. As I write I am aware too of a growing library of books describing the sexual abuse of clients by therapists, from all backgrounds and training. And so we are going from conceal-ment to exposure and both states are inhabited by extreme anxi-ety. In the majority of cases rape is not the main issue. It is an abuse of power of a different character, an abuse of power not accompanied necessarily by physical intimidation. Rather what is being experienced is an abuse of emotional influence and then, of course, we enter a fog of highly subjective and moralistic confu-sion. In the novel the offending middle-aged man admits to what he has done, but he refuses to confess to a misdemeanour. The consequences for him are enormous and devastating. As a psychotherapist I am of course intrigued as to the origins of this sexual misdemeanour. Why has this educated, sophisticated man conducted such a seduction? And who was seducing whom? What was he trying to achieve in the presence of Eros? Why does he fail to defend himself effectively to ward off the consequences of his actions? These are pertinent questions which should inter-est men and women, young and old.

In the case of offending therapists, what happens to drive them to commit professional misconduct of such seriousness? Their professional standing is prejudiced the moment the sexual behav-iour is exposed. There is not much point in responding with a generalisation at this point. My view is that sexual development and conduct is deeply embedded in the psychological, social and biological history of every individual human being. It is present in all our social and cultural constructions but it is not solely a product of those conditions. It is fundamentally primitive and present from the day we are born to the day we die. The unfold-ing discovery and exploration of this sexuality becomes a funda-mental influence in the growth and development of human beings. Perhaps the professor in the novel was simply reacting with 'gut feeling' and his young mistress likewise. In this I stand with Freud.

On the other hand one has to be careful not to limit the presence of sex in the human personality merely to that which is felt as attraction between human beings leading to specific sexual activity between them, especially intercourse. Nowadays we are very well aware of the presence of sexual feeling as an aspect of many cultural activities. This is particularly evident in the case of the visual and performance arts in all their forms.

Example

> *Diana, a member of a large band, played the clarinet. She led a complex sexual life. In therapy she admitted to her lust. She would fancy a man, knowing nothing about him. The gut feeling of lust would take over and that was that. On the other hand she also explained that when she played a clarinet solo with her big band, and she stood up to play, the feeling of sexual arousal would flood her being and she would rise and fall on her heels as the beauty of the sound poured forth to an expectant and adoring audience. An act of sexual communication was taking place both within and without her presence as an artist.*

I would add that sexual activity is deeply woven into many other human expressions and plays a colourful part in framing our interpersonal social responses, without us being especially aware of the sexual origins of the experience. If this is so then psychotherapists will have to reckon with the phenomenon within the relationship with their clients and nowhere could this be more true than in the encounter in the privacy of the therapy room. Many years ago, sitting having a pleasant lunch with a psychoanalyst and his wife, I was intrigued when the wife began to talk about her fantasies that occurred when her husband therapist went into the therapy room with an attractive young woman client. My wife was present and, as I was on the point of entering therapy training, I was pleased that our lunch companion was discussing sexual feelings in such an open and frank manner. The analyst husband listened too with close attention to his wife's conversation. I think some of it was new to him. For both of them the subject was very important. They had both left earlier marriages in favour of each other. I knew that it would be important to my wife as I embarked on a career as a psychoanalytical psychotherapist. She, too, might find herself wondering about the secrecy of the therapy room and hopefully share her feelings with me.

No one can prescribe what a psychotherapist does with this awareness other than to acknowledge its influence and construct a consciousness that allows it to be taken into account in various ways. The most obvious setting for attention is in the supervision time. But I am a firm believer in self-supervision and a close scrutiny of the self in the role of therapist is, in my view, an on-going imperative for all psychotherapists and counsellors. We owe this scrutiny to our clients but most of all to ourselves.

Example

James, a homosexual man, became my client. I held a conventional liberal view of homosexual behaviour, believing it was within the range of sexual behaviour of many human beings. I thought that as with heterosexuality, it would throw up problems that were derived from early sexual development and experienced in current relationships, including the one with me. I determined, therefore, to work in an open way with my 'gay' clients, acknowledging the legitimacy of their sexual orientation, whilst at the same time regarding their sexual life as available to scrutiny, as any other aspect of their being. I was also very aware too that homosexuality is not clearly or firmly bound by a particular sexual act or choice of partner. I knew that I had been attracted to men and boys when I was a young boy and man growing up. I had enjoyed a friendship with a gay male couple, one a musician and the other a writer, when I was acting with a fringe theatre company in London. I was only twenty years old. Their sexuality was blatant, engaging, amusing and threatening, even dangerous at a time when homosexual behaviour was illegal. So when this male gay client came to me I knew and acknowledged that he would take me back to a relationship experienced fifty years ago. I had never felt the need or desire to sexualise my relationship with these old friends, but I had found them immensely attractive as artists and human beings. I had never felt disturbed by their choice of sexual activity. But on occasion when we argued with one another I had to defend my heterosexual choice of girlfriends with vigour.

This helped me a good deal with James and we talked easily enough about issues of behaviour such as buggary and fellatio and his problems with sexual realisation within a gay culture. He was especially caught up with Internet and telephone sex and sometimes very worried by what he sometimes experienced as an addiction. A former therapist had suggested the idea of addiction to him. I felt his goodwill and commitment to therapy and these feelings were not limited to transference activity. Similarly, I 'liked' James without anxiety about inappropriate attachment. To some extent he was a figure of pleasant counter-transference. I think his choice of me, a man, as a therapist was useful for him and me. But bearing in mind the prevalence of homophobia in our society, it was important that I should not over-compensate in the relationship for any discrimination he might experience in his social and professional life.

There are many men and women who react strongly when faced with a homosexual person within their private or professional lives. Such reaction is complex and variable and needs to be addressed both by the person feeling it and the gay person on the receiving end of their projections. A good example of a worrying aspect within psychotherapy itself is the present-day reluctance of some psychoanalytical training bodies to allow gay people to train as therapists. Sometimes the condition of training is that the gay trainee addresses what is described as his or her sexual pathology, i.e. homosexuality, in therapy. The implications are obvious. The sexual disposition is pathologised.

On the other hand, it also seems clear that homosexual men and women have to face whatever is within themselves that has brought them to reject sexual intimacy with the opposite sex. Sometimes it is obvious that the superficial surface of acceptance on both sides of the sexual divide is merely a defence against anger, anxiety, hurt and hatred.

Finally we all, as human beings, seek to find and protect an identity, and our sexual orientation and disposition is central to that search. A good part of our work as psychotherapists is concerned with helping our clients to realise themselves and find a way of being that meets perfectly legitimate desires for personal fulfilment, in whatever manner that attracts them most. Their sexual identity is central to that search and to become fully realised sexually within their gender is to achieve deep satisfaction.

In closing this chapter I just want to go back to the beginning where I suggested that transference is an everyday occurrence.

Example

> *I was in a social situation in a neighbour's house, talking to an intelligent attractive woman in her early seventies. We were talking about a course she was following at the local university and she suddenly said: 'Well, yes I am enjoying it, the other students are a smashing lot, but the tutor!' She paused and looked slightly worried. 'Well, she is a lot younger than me and for some reason I think she doesn't like me very much, and I don't like that. It's never happened to me before like this. I find it quite disturbing.' I found myself, without thinking very much, blurting out: 'Maybe she hates her mother.' My neighbour grinned at me: 'Well, as a matter of fact she told us that on more than one occasion.'*

Enough said.

3 The Rules of the Game

As soon as I wrote this chapter heading I realised I was entering a difficult field of discussion. In what sense could therapy be classified as a game? Wasn't it essentially belittling to suggest that therapy was a game? I can imagine the little gasps of horror coming from some of my overly serious colleagues, for whom I sometimes think psychotherapy has become a sort of religion, a whole belief system, capable of addressing all the most profound human questions. I have noticed that the notion of spirituality, with all its ambiguous resonance, is becoming a central concern for some therapists and their clients. So to use such a term as 'game' to describe what may go on in the therapy room seems to court dispute, even disgust. My *Pocket Oxford Dictionary* devotes a lengthy piece to defining and describing the word 'game'. It talks of frivolity, fun, jest; it speaks of the game as a scheme; one thinks of a plot, then 'the game is up', revealed. One can think of 'game' as another name for 'profession': 'Actually, I am in the psychotherapy game,' I heard myself revealing at a neighbour's party, and immediately felt a bit worried at what might be thought to be trivialising my activity as a therapist. I need not have worried as my listener followed up this remark with perfectly sensible enquiries. At least I hadn't inadvertently said that 'I was on the game'. One of the most intriguing expressions in the dictionary is the word 'gamesmanship'. It is defined as the 'art of winning games by psychological advantage'. This opens up a whole gamut of possibilities. Who has the advantage in the therapy room? One would imagine it to be the therapist.

In my final appraisal of the word I well remember the word 'game' being used as a lofty expression of virtue when a hero might be described as struggling to win in the great game of life. It is not a fashionable expression now but as a teenager I associated it with the need to face a challenge and engage in a struggle to understand the rules of the game and then to enter into the engagement without fear, hoping always to succeed. It is this latter sense of the term 'game' that I refer to in the title of this chapter. I was somewhat reassured when a distinguished psychoanalyst assessing my proposal for this book, although critical of a number of the proposed features, found the suggestiveness of the concept of 'game' interesting.

Example

> *Christine came to see me depressed and puzzled about the shape and condition of her life. At one level she could be seen as an accomplished and successful professional psychologist but at another she had a sense of herself as a failure, one who avoided issues, who used her psychological training to evade relationships with others and, most importantly, herself. Our early sessions were difficult as she tried to establish her professional rules in the therapy room rather than the rules that I followed as a psychotherapist. She was very bright and well trained in her profession, and that was part of the problem. Her rules of discourse, engagement, were different from mine and she was reluctant to unlearn them in the psychoanalytic therapy room. On the contrary, her academic education had given her a set of intellectual references, a set of rules, by which to communicate and hence learn. The psychoanalytic framework did not enter her schema very easily and, to some extent, had been consciously disregarded, undermined and proscribed by her university tutors. Psychotherapy and its dialogue was not seen as objective or scientific and could not be seen as useful to the study of psychology. So 'playing the game' to a new set of rules in therapy was hard work for her. Fortunately, there was an element in the therapy room that helped her to establish a discourse with me: the transference element. This element had not been dismissively addressed in her psychology degree course – indeed it was simply absent as a significant psychological fact; but she soon found that its presence emerged in therapy. I treated it as a golden rule to work with it and she began to do so as well. We engaged with the transference phenomenon with vigour. She soon came to accept the importance of this rule in the therapy game, resisting her 'resistance', and she observed it attentively, not only by addressing its presence in the therapy room but in the world outside as well.*

I will discuss this example further at a later point in this chapter but for the moment would ask the reader to acknowledge that here is an instance of a rule being invoked and worked within a positive therapeutic way. This particular rule is central to the 'game' of psychoanalytic psychotherapy. The game is a serious one that can be lost by either participant and, unlike a game of ping-pong, it would then have serious consequences for all concerned.

Another 'rule' is on the subject of disclosure. I ask clients to be as open and frank as possible and to avoid personal censorship in all the circumstances of therapy. They are assured that the therapy room is inviolable and that I shall not reveal their personal secrets to third parties. All this is agreed to and we work together in a spirit of openness and trust. But having said that I also have to recognise how well certain clients can manoeuvre to withhold important information. I am thinking of a particular male client.

Example

David is a busy, self-employed entrepreneur. He sells his expert advice to a number of wealthy businesses for good fees. He is well established, even sought after, commercially and professionally successful. He is a family man. When he came to me it was to propose therapy to help his personal development, especially in relation to his sex life which was virtually absent in his relationship with his partner – at 40 years of age this seemed to be an issue to be addressed. A further problem was his occasional disabling depression. Of course, it was pretty obvious that the two difficulties were related to each other. It was quite remarkable the way in which David could agonise over infidelities and masturbatory adventures on the Internet without relating these experiences to his relationship with his partner at all. Indeed, he spoke fondly and indulgently of her. He liked to sleep with her and found her naked physical presence in bed with him a comforting and sensually delightful experience. But they did not make love in any sexually explicit way. As for his children, they got very little mention in his talk in the therapy room. He seemed very loving and concerned with them but they rarely appeared in his discussion as dynamic figures in the foreground of his emotional life.

When I pointed this out he would somewhat reluctantly agree with me and promise to address the issues of these ephemeral emotional figures with more energy. But this commitment would soon fade away. I found it exhausting and confusing as a therapist constantly having to be held in a state of extra alertness when I noticed that these key figures had slipped out of the frame once more. What most excited his attention were his work and his sexual misdemeanours (as he saw them). The problem for me was to avoid allowing the legitimacy of these topics, interesting, even compelling as they were, to dominate the therapeutic encounters. He was undoubtedly unwittingly censoring other proper material for the therapy room. Paradoxically he was censoring what he thought of as 'safe' material in favour of what he thought of as 'dangerous' material. He was breaking a rule of the game! To not play the game occurs as much from omission as from positive manoeuvres to cover up and hide difficult material. It is a form of defence. It occurred to me that if he gave attention to his own family he would stir up memories and feelings concerning his family of origin and he wanted to avoid this. It was as if he displayed the erotic material of his misdemeanours in the therapy room in order to interest me and keep me focussed on his 'here and now', rather than his past. I was patient and worked steadily towards his emotional history but there were moments when I despaired of our progress.

The above experience falls clearly into the area of resistance. In psychoanalytic psychotherapy 'resistance' is an accepted phenomenon that has to be addressed and resolved if good therapy is to progress. Sometimes when working with a client it is possible to experience the twists and turns of the client's words that seek to obscure or disguise the pathology of their emotional world. The therapist has a sense of being drawn into a 'game' like chess where one opponent seeks to outwit and frustrate the approach of the other. Experiencing the frustration of this situation is relieved when it becomes possible to bring the client to a realisation of checkmate. The obscuration is defeated and the client comes to see the nature of the neurotic ploys that have worked so powerfully to impede her progress in therapy. The game is resolved in favour of therapy.

Games are associated with roles. The humanistic psychotherapies acknowledge role and role-play without difficulty.

However, it should be noted that some therapists, for example Yalom (1975), express powerful reservations. Yalom's main concern appears to be with the idea of the individual being identified within particular role heterogeneity and held there. He writes this in relation to group therapy where it is possible to attach role performance to an individual member in a rigid expectation, which may become self-fulfilling. In psychodrama, where I trained for some years (Feasey, 2001), it is argued that our lives are lived out in a series of roles that we play, either skilfully or clumsily. Playing the roles has to be learned and much of the learning takes place in childhood when we practise assiduously in order to gain the status of role achievement. In response to Yalom's reservations I would suggest that the key concept here is that as individuals we are capable of playing any number of roles, as they are evoked by a personal or social situation. Indeed, to some extent our role flexibility is a measurement of our mental health. Our ability to drop a role, as well as assume one, is a pretty vital test of our capacity to cope with the demands made upon us in an increasingly complex social and emotional world.

Although some therapists may not agree, it can be argued quite convincingly that in our training as therapists we learn the rules of our life game as psychotherapists. We implement these rules with our clients, who, in turn, learn the rules of client behaviour that relate to our form of psychotherapy. Indeed, Luepnitz (2003) describes this process vividly, admiringly describing how Lacan came to challenge the process of training experiences which creates psychotherapists who, almost unwittingly, perpetuate uncritically the values and forms of the training body. She is concerned with the process of 'becoming' a therapist but here I am arguing that there is a profound consequence for the client/patient who 'becomes' a psychotherapy patient/client. This occurrence was cleverly and tellingly parodied in the comedy drama *Auf Weidersein Pet*, BBC 1 (2004). In this comic drama one character plays a working-class man becoming a 'client' and another becomes the 'therapist' to great humorous effect. Through this process we too, readers of this book, could be described as entering into roles as therapist and client. These roles are best played to our advantage when we understand what is required of us, in other words the rules of the game.

Some of the rules we live by as therapists or counsellors are quite obvious and define our presence in the clients' lives.

Important Basic 'Good' Rules of Therapy

1. We strive to offer our clients unconditional regard.
2. We offer a confidential relationship.
3. We practise an understandable form of psychotherapy or counselling (to the client) and undertake to do no harm to our clients.
4. We undertake not to unfairly exploit the relationship with the client to our advantage, financial, emotional, sexual, social or otherwise.
5. We offer a therapeutic contract and observe this until it is mutually closed.
6. We provide a regular regime and within it observe proper attention to time, place and boundaries, both physical and emotional.
7. We undertake to act for the benefit of the client and not someone else.
8. In private practice we negotiate a therapy fee and only change it with consultation with our clients.
9. We provide secure and appropriate accommodation where confidentiality can be observed and therapy safely practised.

There are, of course, 'bad' and more subtle rules that we observe as therapists in the therapy encounter, when a mode of working calls upon us to exercise energy or restraint according to our understanding of the situation within the rules of the game. Furthermore we gradually accustom our clients to behave in a particular way in the therapy situation. This can be likened to a game where the therapist plays in a predictable and appropriate way and the client, with some reservations, does likewise.

With encouragement and some direct instruction the client learns some of the rules of the game. She discovers the therapist's rules and the rules that attach appropriately to her. And so the client and therapist play together.

Example

I talked to Christine in the early assessment encounters about the rules outlined above, some of them directly and some of them by implication. She listened and responded well, only sometimes looking a little impatient as I slowly proceeded, outlining the conditions of therapy as I went along. This slow encounter and its emphasis upon exploration between us were new to her. It was not her custom to work in such a way with her clients and I think she thought it all a bit of a waste of time – 'So why couldn't we just get on with it.' She balked more obviously when I asked her not to come to the sessions prepared with predetermined material to work with and certainly not a list of topics to be covered. This raised her hackles and soon she was deeply involved in a debate about 'resistance'. This led us to talk about the use of the intellect and our cognitive processes of preparation, which we take for granted most of the time, as against the more problematical issue of spontaneous free association and impulse. All this sprang into her mind when I asked her to confront censorship in the sessions and to address impulses to conceal or distract attention in our discourse. She was quite a moralistic young woman and so first of all she did not like the idea that she might harbour thoughts and feelings that would be hard to express in the sessions, and certainly not in normal social situations. Her first reaction was to deny that she ever did censor her thought and feelings, or tell lies, white or otherwise, in her relationships with friends and family. I managed to suppress a sceptical smile.

Readers might have noticed I have emphasised the word 'resistance' here. This word is a good one to think about for a moment or two. It is one of the central assumptions of psychoanalytic psychotherapy that clients will display 'resistance' to a certain course of action or thinking. The therapist 'knows' they are being resistant and calls the experience into consciousness and discussion. Now, obviously, this phenomenon could be true, but it may not be. Indeed, the client's refusal to pursue a particular course of thinking or feeling may be healthily based. I am not saying here that the therapist is always wrong. What I am saying is that the therapist, in relation to the client, needs to consider the possibility of being wrong. I have come to believe that the 'relational' approach to therapy encourages the therapist to avoid a 'bad' rule that insists upon the superior understanding of the therapist, in favour of a more open, dynamic approach, which allows for the normal failures of communication we all encounter as human beings, and that includes therapists!

Sometimes therapists, especially those from the analytic tradition, or counsellors working in a person-centred mode, are accused of ignoring or discouraging material in therapy that relates to essentially contemporary environmental influences. The interesting article 'Are We Allowed to Disagree?' (in *The Critical Journal of Psychology, Counselling and Psychotherapy*) by Paul Moloney (2001) is especially accusing in this respect. However, my view of practice does not suggest to me that there is a rule that says such social material is irrelevant and has to be discarded or prevented from entering the therapeutic conversation. Some psychotherapists such as Gorer (1966) are actually contemptuous of Kleinians who he suggests hold that the internal world of the client, in all its aspects, is independent of class, culture or race and rarely relate in their communication with the actual environment the client exists within. In the case discussed above, the client discovered there was a good deal of frustration and anger in the work situation that was being repressed in favour of 'good professional manners' as she put it. This anger had a depth and energy to it that suggested other associations from her personal history. This meant that our therapy work had to be conducted on two levels: primarily we were concerned with the pathology of these feelings, but (and this was a big but) we also had to address the contemporary experience. She had a particularly difficult colleague who drew out the anger from my client, where it became a kind of repressed misery for her. Much of her historical anger became vested in this professional relationship and it had to be disentangled and revealed. Certainly in the early days of psychoanalysis, when Freud was writing some of his famous case histories, there is no evidence that he attempted to isolate intrapsychic material from environmental and existential material of a social character (see Freud, 1962). Quite the contrary, Freud invariably took into account the family and the contemporary social relations of his patients when framing a diagnosis of their, as he saw it, illness. And so it was necessary to place my client in her social context of work, where many puzzling feelings (to my client) occurred and much distress was experienced, as against the situation in her domestic setting, where there was relative harmony. Obviously, displacement had occurred but the projection settled upon a tricky, ambitious and rival woman at work and this could not be ignored.

I have always been disturbed by the frequent appearance of articles and books that purport to discuss scientifically the types of clients who are able or unable to benefit from psychoanalytic psychotherapy. In other words it is asserted that there are many clients who cannot play the game because they are unable to learn the rules of therapy. I think for the most part this is nonsense and more often than not it simply supports a class-bound approach to therapy. But having said this, it is still a position held by a number of capable and experienced psychotherapists (see, for example, Dryden, 1984) and, of course, psychiatrists. Perhaps it is more difficult for working-class clients to learn the language and social mores of their psychoanalytic psychotherapist. Her language is likely to be markedly different from their own. The therapist often has forms of expression that are different from the client's and there will be gaps in cultural and social experience that will need to be addressed by both sides. This is especially true in the area of morality and social values of all kinds, right down to the kind of food each one eats. It is precisely this issue of 'both sides' that some therapists find difficult. They have learned a mode of professional behaviour and expression which they believe is central to their activity as therapists, and to adapt or alter these modes in favour of a compromise of expression to suit their client is something that some therapists regard as beyond the pale. In terms of game the therapist is apt to approach the encounter with one set of rules and the working-class client with another set. It is not often that the rules are immediately compatible with each other and some negotiation needs to take place as the therapy progresses where both parties modify their position. They learn to play the game with each other and to share a common therapeutic language.

Example

John was one of the most intelligent, under-educated male clients I have ever worked with. He came to me on recommendation from a counsellor who had seen him six times as part of a company-counselling contract. He was described as suffering from depression. To the credit of his counsellor she did not apply any value judgement to his modes of expression, which were sometimes obscene, aggressive and often vivid. He worked in a big business as a highly valued financial consultant, his job was to sort things out and put things right. Sometimes the activity was concrete, removing computer drives and replacing them, writing financial programmes, and sometimes it was almost totally abstract. He was a natural and his lack of formal education seemed not to matter much. I was very aware of this when he came for assessment. He seemed surprised when I pointed out that he was there to assess me as much as I was to assess him. In reality we would assess each other and decide if we could work together. He was not used to this kind of encounter and at first he floundered, lapsing into silence when he felt threatened by an unexpected gesture or remark on my part. Eventually he grew angry and told me I was a 'wanker'. I think he was comparing me to false so-called 'value-free stances' that he sometimes encountered in his work place. The issue was one of trust.

The reader will notice that I used the word 'gesture' in the previous paragraph. I was aware he was very observant of my body posture and his too was quite vivid and revealing. From the very beginning of this relationship I felt his presence in the therapy room in a manner not normally experienced. His body language was powerful and I felt my body responding to his. He would slouch into the therapy room and flop into the large armchair that was on offer. He scorned the sofa with a look and never voluntarily referred to its presence. He would twist his body away from me, disassociating and distancing himself from any suggestion of closeness. He came believing that another half dozen or so sessions would do the trick – whatever the 'trick' was! His depression was contained and primarily expressed in anger, which showed itself in personal loathing and disgust. He frequently went on drinking binges with 'mates', getting hopelessly drunk or picking up women in pubs who were of little concern to him and for whom he was no more than what he described as a 'good fuck' (although I wondered how 'good' he was when he had drunk so much).

He was the young and loving father of a toddler girl and a six-month-old baby boy but, when he came to me, his wife had thrown him out of the expensive family home. The loss of the house did not appear to be of any real concern to him but the loss of his children was a deadly blow to his self-esteem. He loved his wife too, or so he claimed when entering therapy, and despite the separation they often met and had sexual intercourse together which he claimed was 'terrific'. He was puzzled by his own behaviour; he described it as not 'playing the game' with his wife and he thought she was justified in 'kicking him out'. His mates thought she was probably justified while at the same time describing her as a bitch, someone who 'did not know when she was well off'. Most of John's deepest anger was reserved for his in-laws. He was particularly incensed by his father-in-law who was a 'do-it-yourself' man. This meant he was always at the family home doing jobs that John's wife wanted doing but would not entrust to her husband. He in turn saw her as a daddy's girl and it was not long before he began to admit to jealousy and fury, feeling that he sometimes did not come first in his wife's emotional response when her father came into the frame of her life. John's lack of formal education, his complete ignorance of familiar psychological terms and formulations, did not prove an intractable difficulty in confronting this classic Oedipal family construct. As he put it, referring to his father-in-law: 'The bastard has cut off my balls.' At a later stage he grew interested in the fact that he was almost completely out of touch with his feelings concerning his own violent father and the persecution he had suffered at his father's hands during his early childhood. His mother hardly interested him at all. In his view she was just stupid; he despised her materialistic values and interests. The main gain for John in this therapy was his increased interest and curiosity concerning his emotional life both in its inner and outer manifestations.

I was satisfied that within three months, on a once a week basis, John had learned to play a good game with sufficient skill to enable him to examine his life and relationships with growing sensitivity and insight. I hoped and believed he would be enabled to address and make good destructive elements in his psychological and social behaviour. He started from a place where he had to learn some fundamental requirements of the therapy game.

- He had to learn to tolerate openness and frankness in the therapy room;
- he was learning to listen to himself, achieving some measure of detachment from the primitive feelings that welled up in him;
- he had to find a vocabulary that adequately described feelings, felt by himself and others, in a descriptive non-abusive way;
- he had to discover the meaning of the narrative of his life, and cease fragmenting experiences as if they had no connection with one another.

He had to learn that I was a player too, not merely a hander-out of prescriptions for good living, and that I could be trusted to (as Sir Henry Newbolt put it in his poem 'Vitai Lampada') 'Play up! Play up! and play the game.'

Within a relatively short time-frame these aspects of psychotherapy became active in the therapy room and I felt confident that we could work creatively together. To quote Christopher R. Stones (2003), he had learned in the transference situation that although I was approachable, responsive and concerned for him, that 'I am not your friend. I am your therapist. But I am a friendly therapist.' One of our biggest problems was his haste. By nature he worked professionally in a speedy and effective manner and he found the pace of therapy bewildering and its slow measured movement frustrating. Initially he was looking for a 'quick fix', as he put it. We had to learn to pace each other in response to our different 'natural' rhythms of work. So as he slowed down I picked up a bit more speed.

My feeling was that a classic diagnostic psychotherapy interview would have almost certainly rejected John as a potential client. Indeed, it is probable that he would have dismissed such an interview as being useless, not of any value to him therapeutically. Following the medicalisation of many psychoanalytic and psychodynamic procedures in hospitals, clinics and training centres, the diagnostic approach with its emphasis on naming and categorisation sometimes inhibits creative and therapeutic exploration between client and therapist.

To name a disease in some respects is valuable and reassuring in the field of physical medicine but it has little place in psychotherapy and counselling. Indeed, it can be a positive hindrance to good creative work. A good example of naming that has brought nothing but confusion in its place is the expression 'personality disorder', suggestive of basis organic dysfunction rendering the victim untreatable. It has virtually no useful meaning in the realm of psychotherapy and counselling, and it is not a useful term in the great game of therapy, concealing as it does more than it reveals. Craig Newnes (1999) demonstrates convincingly that the so-called scientific approach to mental health that attempts to locate severe psychological disturbance (mental illness) in dysfunctional brain tissue activity is wrong and misleading. There is no known physiological test, such as a blood test, which is able to reveal the cause of such an illness. There is no objective evidence known to psychiatry. This emphasis on finding scientific evidence is driven, in my view, by the medical profession's wishes always to put a name to a pathological condition. Without a name for the illness the doctor often feels helpless. I fear that some of the psychotherapy training in a medical milieu may well be drifting down this blind alley. Of course, this process is sometimes disguised in the therapy culture by describing it differently, for example as 'needing to find a formulation before therapy can begin'.

And so one of the rules of the game in psychotherapy and counselling is to avoid dependence on naming a human psychological condition, even where we are very tempted to do so. We must put aside psychological shorthand, such as naming people as depressives, schizophrenics, paranoid personality disorder types, manic depressives, well neurotics and so on. The rule of labelling must be put aside as a bad rule. The rule rather is to work with the client in exploring the condition of the psychological experience, relating it always to the unique world of the client both in its psychological and social presentation. We can know, for example, that a client has a great fear of the outdoors and clings to the safety of the home, and that many would call this condition agoraphobia. And then what? We have a name but are we any further forwards in understanding the nature of the experience for the client? It could be argued that the labelling process is useful to professional therapists as a shorthand, enabling quick communication. However, I still remain sceptical and fearful of the outcome when clients and patients become a label rather than a person. This is a particular danger in hospital and clinic settings.

Example

Maria was an attractive, intelligent and well-educated Italian woman who came to me for help. She was married, apparently very happily to an artist who was successful, caring and attentive to her needs. So what was the problem? She made an appointment to see me by telephone. The doorbell rang and I opened it to be confronted by her and her husband. I was surprised. He smiled in a friendly way and said, 'I'll be on my way. What time should I come back and collect her?' Frankly, I was astonished and taken aback. Marie looked anxiously at me and said to him, 'Come back in fifty minutes.' I knew then that this was not her first time seeing a psychotherapist. She knew about the fifty-minute hour. Actually, this is a convention I do not observe. A rule that I felt had no force, a mere historical product of habit and convention. Not a valid rule of the game. Nevertheless her remark had conveyed to me a lot of meaning here on the doorstep. I was also struck by his expression 'come and collect her' rather than 'come and collect you'. He had addressed the remark to me rather than her and she had noticed this and been rather embarrassed by it. She was being left and she would be collected, like an infant school child – certainly not like an adult. This immediately impacted on the therapy situation. My preference is always to address the client as an adult even where the person is expressing very infantile feelings and so it meant that this material would come from the doorstep into the therapy room at this first session of mutual exploration.

In the room she spoke of suffering from agoraphobia as if the term would explain everything about her husband's presence and his remark. Of course it did not. There was much work to be done. I mentioned her suggestion of her husband coming back in fifty minutes. She immediately began to tell me about her psychoanalysis in Rome some years ago and the use of fifty minutes for the session. I knew we were facing a complex situation. I explained my own practice and remarked at the manner in which we had been thrown into the 'deep end' as it were, within minutes of her arrival at my door.

If I had played the wrong game, as this young woman arrived, and accepted her diagnosis of her difficulties as being vested in agoraphobia, I would have found myself treading a limited path and perhaps the wrong one, or certainly a long one from which a diversion would have eventually been made. For the moment I ignored her self-diagnosis and pursued the matter of her reference to psychoanalysis and what she expected from me. The result of this enquiry was complex and interesting. She had received psycho-analysis in Rome at the instigation of a male cousin who himself was a psychoanalyst of the Kleinian school. He had seduced her when she was a teenager. All this was revealed in a flat, detached manner in the first session, not so much as to deny her feelings but rather to set an example of her ability to talk openly about events that were in themselves deeply questionable and confusing. It was as if for the moment she was the therapist and I a mere observer. Two other issues then quickly surfaced. The first was the question of her feelings and her tendency to intellectualise her experience and the second was that she was accustomed to interpretations occupying the prime place in the therapy sessions. That had been the rules of the game in Rome with her analyst. Now she had to learn a new rule in her work with me. As a psychoanalytic psychotherapist I, too, respect the place of interpretation in ther-apy. The rule, however, that I put in place was that it would be her, the client, who had the guiding role in the process of inter-pretation. The onus was on me to assist her in the process. My opening gambit was always the same, to ask her to try to make more than one sense of the material she was offering me; to make personal interpretations and examine them critically. From that we could construct a dialogue of enquiry and response. The issue of 'interpretation' is a vivid one in psychoanalytical psychother-apy, and many clients have written critical accounts of feeling that understanding has been forced upon them by therapists insisting on a certain interpretation of something said in a ther-apy session (see Sands, 2000). But interpretation is a common-place activity and how many times have we heard someone say: 'Well, I wonder what she meant by saying that?' The issue is always: 'Who does the interpretation?'

On one occasion a very important aspect of herself was revealed this way. She had mentioned, almost with pride, that she and her husband did not rely on chemical or barrier contracep-tion. Rather they enjoyed a frequent sexual intercourse based on 'withdrawal' as the preferred way of avoiding pregnancy. I asked her to think about the statement and to think about it as a communication to me and to herself and what meaning it may convey apart from the factual information. Soon she began to associate it with dependence on her husband, the abandonment of her personal power and possibly the wish for a baby 'accidentally' conceived. This latter point was very important for she was potentially the greater money earner. His life as an artist was economically precarious. She suspected he would see an unplanned pregnancy as a disaster.

Some months later the therapy was terminated. We had never spoken of agoraphobia but as a symptom it had simply disappeared, almost uncommented upon. But the story was not quite over. Months after Maria left my care I was standing outside a local hi-fi shop, enjoying a fantasy about owning a superb and outrageously expensive pair of loudspeakers, when Maria was suddenly by my side. She was pushing a small pram. I turned on hearing her voice, and immediately saw this new born baby. She looked at me and said: 'Well, what do you think of your baby Mr Therapist?', and before I could respond she continued, 'I am on maternity leave; nowadays I am Head of Languages at the comprehensive school.' She paused and before I could find the right thing to say she gave me a grin, 'Well, I'll leave you in peace. Cheerio, as they say here in England.' And then she was gone. Shortly afterwards I left the town with my family to live in a large city. I have never seen her since, although her child will now be at least a teenager, and there's a thought: was it a boy or a girl? I shall probably never know. But our game, although very contained and prescribed, was fruitful. It had been a good game and the rules had been sensible ones.

Boundaries

I wish to close this chapter with a special discussion on boundaries. In many discussions of boundaries between therapists and counsellors it is often seen in the context of the fear of a client or patient breaking boundaries, and in a sense, breaking out of the patient role in which the highly complex game of therapy is played. Sometimes it is discussed as if it were almost a disciplinary matter and the client is seen as misbehaving. It might be said that the client is 'acting out' whereas it would have been more appropriate to use the American term 'acting up', meaning to defy the constrictions and directions applied by authority (e.g. in this setting, this would be the therapist). Undoubtedly this occasionally happens but rarely, in my view, is it appropriate to see it in this way. When I think of the boundary of therapy I tend to view it in a more progressive and creative manner. The primary aim of a therapeutic boundary is to place the client in a secure situation where virtually anything can be said, and any discussion can take place without recourse to the normal restrictions of polite or considerate behaviour on the part of the client. Freud especially emphasised the importance of these boundaries and linked the approach to the issue of confidentiality, which is a tricky one, especially in the health service (both public and private). His injunction to patients (as he described them) was to speak aloud everything and anything that came into their mind in therapy without censorship. This was a unique injunction, and for his contemporaries it might have seemed a shocking suggestion to make to a patient.

Although his particular words are now rarely used, there is an assumption in therapy and counselling practice that censorship should be abolished in the therapeutic encounter. Obviously this is, for the most part, rarely achieved to any total degree. None of us are capable of such a risky activity, to any total exposure of our secret inner world of longing, whether it is for good or ill. But at least we try as clients and as therapists. The paradox of the boundary is that, although it constricts the relationship of client and therapist, it also offers a creative and expansive degree of personal freedom of expression to the client and, for the therapist, a place of safely in which to receive controversial information, expressed without the usual social constraint. As is implied by the sub-title of this book a kind of intimacy is set up, but it is an intimacy without inter-relational consequences outside the therapy room.

Example

She was only fourteen years old when she was referred to me for therapy, and she was described as an extravagant and consummate liar. She appeared to be frightening her parents by worrying sexual behaviour which allegedly took place when she went out with her mates on a Friday or Saturday night. At the girls' grammar school she attended she was regarded as a good, middle ability pupil presenting no obvious cause for concern in either her behavior or her attitude of compliance with school mores and discipline. Her mother was 'worried sick' and her father confessed to roaming the streets of the local market town late at night when she was out with her 'mates' on the razzle dazzle, as he put it. Her appearance in front of me after school in her school uniform was a portrait of modest decorum, her clothes were always clean and tidy; her long socks brilliantly white. She sat in this decorous state in front of me and waited to be 'told off' for telling her parents, and especially her father, these terrible stories of sexual adventure, the cause of such extreme anxiety. However I was to disappoint her in this respect. Did she expect me to believe them? I listened quietly and attentively to her lurid accounts of her sexuality and rarely commented other than to clarify a detail from time to time; I made it clear by my body language that I was interested. Eventually, exasperated with my position, she announced that I should say something because everything she had told me was lies. I said that I knew this to be so but I found her lies really interesting and I would be pleased to discuss them when she was ready to do so. I would wait upon her in this respect. She burst out laughing. From then on she began to recognise the advantage of the therapy space, in terms of time and place. She began to use the creative boundary.

Her lies became rather like dreams or fantasies, made and described as a means to understanding deeply felt personal needs, which were focussed upon her relationship with her mother and father, and especially the latter. The boy lovers she invented were simply placed as pathways for us to follow, to reach her more deeply experienced Oedipal tensions that she only half felt and, until therapy, did not understand in any way. They simply frightened her.

4 Money . . . for What it's Worth*

Nothing is intrinsically valuable; the value of everything is attributed to it from outside the thing itself, by people.
(John Barth, *The Floating Opera*, 1956)

He that has nothing but merit to support him is in a fair way to starve.
(Anon, eighteenth-century proverb)

Those who have some means think that the most important thing in the world is love. The poor know that it is money.
(Gerard Brenan, 'Thoughts in a Dry Season', 1978)

There is one advantage of being poor – a doctor will cure you faster'.
(Kin Hubbarb, *Ahe Martin's Sayings*, 1915)

As I approached the end of preparing the typescript for this book, one of the publisher's reviewers said: 'Well, what about money?' Indeed what about it? I know I have referred to it obliquely throughout this book, but why not do a full frontal attack on the subject? Am I dodging the issue? Am I inhibited at talking about this, the most taboo of subjects? When did any reader last go to a dinner party or lunch when people openly discussed their earnings?

This article has come from talking to a number of trainees in analytic psychotherapy who as a part of their training are required to treat a number of clients, under supervision, and produce the usual number of assessment statements and formulations together with prognostications concerning the likely approach to therapy and its possible aims and outcomes. As well as this, they are required to write case studies that demonstrate a familiarity with psychoanalytic theory and practice. The essence

---

* A version of this chapter appeared in *Changes Journal*, 3:2 (Autumn 2002).

of the experience is the learning of skills of treatment for the client, leading to a positive outcome. After all, like doctors, the very least that should be required of a psychotherapist is that no harm should be done.

In the field of psychoanalysis there has been a long tradition that trainees take on clients for analysis during training and that the would-be analyst is supervised during the treatment. The economic basis of this activity was that the trainee should get a reward in the form of fees from the client and that this money could then be used to help towards meeting training expenses, which are considerable. Such has been the prevalence of this tradition that it might be said that some 'training psychoanalysts' make most of their income from this training activity. To a limited extent this is true in the training of analytic psychotherapists. Certainly I have offered supervision and therapy to trainees who have been able to earn some money during their training from private clients 'in therapy'. I have then gained tangible benefit in the form of fees from the trainees and the arrangement has been mutually satisfactory. Mind you, it has also been described as 'fleas upon the back of fleas upon the back of fleas . . .'!

Certainly, for me, earning fees from both individual and group therapy was an important way of my meeting my own training expenses, which have been considerable over the years. However, now a relatively new phenomenon has appeared. Some training institutes, attached closely to NHS or private hospitals/psychotherapy centres, are providing clients for trainees who need training experience and supervision but requiring them to work without any remuneration. The unpaid trainees are effectively earning substantial treatment fees for the institutes concerned and, in addition, they are paying considerable training fees to these same institutes. The clients may be paying privately for the treatment, or their insurers are doing so for them, or the referring GP practice is bearing the cost on its practice budget. Obviously the precise arrangements are reflective of the current market situation applying to the providers and purchasers, to use the hideous marketing jargon! Now whatever the justice or fairness of the situation (and clearly there are arguments about the propriety of the arrangement I have described), the individual transaction of money between the therapist and the client is entirely lost in this situation, and with that is lost a whole range of emotional meaning concerning the transference and non-transference relationship of client to therapist and vice versa.

The opening sentence in Chapter 1 of Dorothy Rowe's recent book *The Real Meaning of Money* is as follows: 'The love of money, so St Paul told Timothy, is the root of all evil. If this is true then most of us are evil because most of us do love money.' For some psychotherapists the notion of the psychotherapeutic relationship as being a transaction involving money is quite intolerable. They argue that treatment should be free and offered according to need, not means. This is the central argument relating to the idea of a free National Health Service. The trainees who hold this view will almost certainly try to find employment in the public health and social services. Although I go a long way with this argument I always have nagging away at the back of my mind that old American saying 'There is no such thing as a free lunch'. Liam Clarke (1998) makes the point that some analysts measure the commitment to therapy (on the part of a patient) 'by issues surrounding the money to be paid'. In the same article he points to the deterioration of his relationship with his analytical therapist when they started to haggle over money owing for arranged sessions that did not take place (because Liam had failed to turn up for an appointment where, I suppose, the date had been previously agreed). The error was cumulative but I have no doubt that in the mind of the therapist there would have been considerable interpretative speculation concerning the 'meaning' of the dispute. Clearly in a 'free' health service where there is no real or symbolic money transaction between therapist and patient then it could be argued 'resistance' behaviour of the kind described by Clarke would be that much more difficult to confront. However, it might be argued that it would probably arise in different guises.

As soon as money comes into a transaction then the notion of value also enters the scene. As John Barth argues: 'Value is attributed – no value is intrinsic'. Thus value is demonstrated on the part of the client by 'paying' the therapist for her time and skilful attention; where actual money changes hands this relationship is very clear. Furthermore, the therapist then may be judged as offering good or bad value for the money offered.

In psychoanalytic terms money is linked with faeces. The product of the child's effort is shown with pride by the child to their mother: 'Look mummy, a big, big jobs.' The mother is expected to be pleased and praise them for what they have done. We see something of a parallel in vulgar angry attacks on money and wealth when people declare that 'Money is shit!' Yes it is and therefore it is valuable, or at least a way of symbolising and offering and receiving value. The child is pleased and the mother is proud and relieved. Only later is the meaning of this activity extended into the more complex areas of power and control; withholding and gratifying; pleasure and shame. We all know what it is like to suffer from constipation and how that will certainly worry the mother. Power issues then enter the arena.

The problem is that when therapy is apparently free – which of course it never is – then the attribution of value in the therapeutic relationship becomes somewhat mystified. In these circumstances the issue of power emerges. The client is no longer a 'purchaser': the client becomes a 'supplicant'. There are inevitable consequences in this situation which play into the therapeutic relationship and one of the consequences is the imbalance of power between the provider and the supplicant. The supplicant has lost the power to purchase and cannot look for value for money in the manner of a paying customer. The supplicating client has no power of 'hire' and 'fire'. The trainee therapist may be abandoned, simply by the client not turning up, and the invariable response to this is a sense of deprivation and anger on the part of the therapist. Unknown to the client, in this situation the therapist may suffer a significant real loss. This occurs in relation to the demands of her training body, in the form of training hours to be accredited on the path to qualification and eventual registration as a psychotherapist. The trainee may also be nervous of such a departure in case it is then interpreted by his trainers as his failure to 'hold' the client 'well enough'.

Where an employer is paying (or in the case of the trainee not paying) the therapist, a relationship is set up between the therapist and the client of mutual dependency; value is attributed to the life of the relationship. As already stated, the client may or may not be aware that the trainee is a trainee, or even be unclear as to whether the therapist is a medical doctor or not. I know of a number of psychotherapists/psychologists who use the academic title 'Doctor' within a psychotherapeutic relationship with consequent ambiguity and confusion. It seems that clinical psychologists are particularly prone to this manoeuvre. So abandonment by the client is a matter resonating both with intra-psychic and extra-psychic material which will not be addressed, analysed and understood within the therapeutic relationship, because the client is no longer there. Confusing to say the least.Where is the value being placed? With psychotherapy or medicine? And from which withdrawn?

The client in such circumstances attributes value to the therapist and trusts the therapist according to that feeling of value. But what about the therapist? The therapist may 'value' the client on altruistic grounds, but that is a complicated position and leads to many questions that are not easy to answer. On the other hand the trainee therapist may 'value' the client because a 'successful' outcome of therapy will lead to approval from the trainer/supervisors, whereas a failure could be felt as a disaster for the trainee. So a 'good' client is one who will respond and 'work' in the therapeutic relationship, and a 'bad' client is one who turns out not to be 'psychologically minded' enough, or is pathologically resistant or one who fails to 'value' therapy and the therapist, perhaps leaving without warning, or just not turning up for the next appointment.

Where money is open and tangible in the therapeutic relationship then the 'real' relationship of psychotherapy is demonstrated without ambiguity. I once heard a therapist describe his analytic hour as consisting of 55 minutes of love and 5 minutes of hate when the money was handed over at the end of the session. We all know the phrase 'money can't buy you love', which is a widely accepted piece of folk wisdom. Tillett (1998) reminds us that sometimes money buys us hate and aggression which, when experienced, is extremely disturbing to both therapist and client, probably in equal measure. On the other hand, I know it is the practice of some analysts and therapists to send a 'bill' to their clients through the post on a monthly basis – thereby giving some distance to the procedure. The money, 'shit', is removed from the immediacy of the therapeutic encounter, perhaps because it is a bit shameful. After all, we soon learn to treat our faeces as being dirty, whilst at the same time keeping a sense of secret shameful pride in a good performance – a 'TGC' (a thundering good crap). A vulgar truism.

Most of us are very conscious of these mixed feelings in the relationship with our clients or in the relationship with our therapists when we slip into the client role. However, what about the parts of the relationship of which we are not so conscious or remain entirely unconscious. The desire for gratification, for reward, for value in our experience of our clients is deeply embedded in the psyche, and the failure to reach and experience those needs in a satisfactory way will certainly have repercussions in the therapeutic relationship. Most therapists acknowledge these needs as they momentarily come to their attention in the therapeutic relationship when examined in supervision, but these moments are necessarily fleeting and are only partial indicators of more deeply entrenched desires of which we only occasionally and partially are conscious.

The exchange of money in itself does not in any sense 'deal' with these unconscious needs and desires. However, the presence of a value transaction, with all that is implied by it, acts as a conscious prompt to both client and therapist. I remember a woman client, middle aged, still sexually active and attractive to a number of men (including male colleagues she worked with) who, at the end of sessions, would rise and carefully place the fee, in cash, on the mantelpiece. Nothing was said. She did not look at me as she did this. There was a distancing of intimacy. Then one day the blindingly obvious association came to her lips. She giggled and looked at me: 'It's like leaving money for a prostitute after the act; money on the mantelpiece!'

This identification of the therapist with prostitution doesn't strike me as unusual. The client, in private practice, is paying for uncritical attention in which the most intimate of exchanges will be allowed, short of physical contact (although phantasies of sexual encounter may well proliferate). This attention is non-judgemental and only concerned with providing satisfaction to the client and not, in the first place, to the therapist. As far as my client was personally concerned she had had one or two brief afternoon sexual encounters with powerful business men when, after an expensive lunch, the man concerned rented a hotel room in a neighbouring city at some considerable expense and they spent a few hours together enjoying all the forbidden pleasures of illicit sexual play and intercourse. A good deal of money was spent to ensure secrecy and pleasure. She was pleased and proud about that and admitted she would only spend such time with men with plenty of money, big cars and confidence in handling the situation. Paradoxically, the atmosphere was charged with guilt and shame; a transaction of money and sex and the power that goes with it.

The literature on the subject of trainee remuneration is very thin. Jeffery Masson in his book *Final Analysis* speaks in pretty sharp tones about the issue of money for trainees in training therapy:

> At normal hourly charges, five days a week, the expense of being trained was considerable. . . . At any rate, a substantial part of my monthly salary went to pay for analysis. (Jeffrey Masson, 1992, p. 21)

Later in the book he talks anxiously about the position he feels himself to be in:

> An hour of analysis a day, five days a week, comes to a lot of money. Admitting failure would have been costly on all fronts: for my self-esteem, for my professional career, for my personal life and for my finances.

It doesn't seem to have occurred to him that his analyst was in a similar position to him. After all, somebody has to pay the gas bill! Sometimes the 'loss' of a client in private practice is felt very distinctly in the purse. There may be a tendency to postpone the day. The bill has to be paid – this is the reality principle.

The issue of gratification comes up in Masson's book *Final Analysis*. He begins to get angry when he:

> suspect[s] that [the analyst] liked thinking about himself and talking about himself more than he liked talking or thinking about me. Understandably. Except that I was paying him for something other than a mutually satisfying conversation.

Masson wanted to satisfy himself, he wanted to talk, to be listened to, to get it all out, not to be forced to restrain in favour of someone else. There is a tendency to narrow the discussion to the presence of money as a transference symbol, which it undoubtedly is. But in my view it is not confined, in psychotherapeutic terms, to that role. It has force in the extra-psychic and intra-psychic world of all of us. The presence of money in the intra-psychic world has to be taken into account. Partly it invites us to regress to the infant stage of production and creativity, it becomes the plastic, creative material that we have moved from the deepest interior of our body to the outside world. We made it. Created it. It is to be treasured and admired. Its smell and presence pleases us and always will do so as we grow towards adulthood. Money and 'shit' stand closely together in our inner world of fantasy, dreams and sexuality. Our early developmental narcissism and sexual awareness is advanced and developed by this intimate association.

The failure of contemporary writers to accord money with the multiplicity of layered meanings it is capable of holding, is a characteristic of the published work I have found in preparing this chapter. For example, John Marzillier (1996) writes quite an interesting article on the subject of money, and notes too the evasiveness of psychotherapists in writing and discussing the subject. However, his personal observations, although attractive, throw very little light on the subject in respect of its powerful metaphoric and symbolic presence in therapy. He dismisses the psychoanalytic view and swings off into a discussion of the subject from a sociological and social psychological position. But his main problem is the usual one of setting one view up against another in rivalrous tension. So the social emphasis in his article is advanced with favour as against the psychoanalytical position. However, we all know that metaphoric and symbolic meaning can exist and flourish alongside realistic social determinants. They are not exclusive positions to hold in rivalry against one another. Indeed such a position of rivalry should be avoided if the rich truthful complexity of the presence of money in our lives is to be understood. Unfortunately, academic psychology often does exactly that – it promotes rivalry and insists upon exclusive 'rightness'. A personal anecdote will suffice to illustrate my point. Growing up and coming to the age of drinking in a small rural community in Devon during the Second World War, I was very pleased to be invited by a soldier cousin (a survivor of the hell of

Dunkirk, the 'War in the Desert' and the Normandy landings) to have a drink with him. We went, a small gang of us into the pub. As we entered, Gerald, another soldier, suddenly said to my cousin: 'Set me up for a pint, I'm going for a slash.' As he walked away the other men grinned and laughed to each other. I was puzzled in my naivety. I couldn't see what there was to laugh at. My cousin gave a savage kind of grin, looked at me, saw my bewilderment and explained: 'Oh, he's always been a tight-arsed git. But we'll get him later on, you'll see.'

This crude and coarse language incorporates the Freudian view, which has so entered the common culture that its origins are quite unknown to those who use the concepts. The concept remains active and live because it conveys an acknowledged truth. This issue is about holding on and retaining. Not an exclusive truth, but one that nevertheless serves a good purpose in the process of human communication. Cognitive psychologists often miss this view in either dismissal or avoidance of the Freudian position.

All these matters are dramatised in the most concrete and symbolic way by the exchange of money. In the NHS where no direct payment occurs, the 'value relationship' of therapist and client is not so easily located and the symbol is metamorphosed in a manner that can lead to obscurity. Hanging on to a client, getting rid of or letting go a client takes on a rather different meaning, and the absence of an obvious and pressing value transaction may make it more difficult to trace the meaning of these states of being. Often, in the NHS, the 'cost' of therapy is represented by time and attention. I know of a clinic where the client may be allowed a year of treatment, the maximum time allowed, and this is decided in advance of therapy commencing. I cannot think of any NHS treatment programme in physical medicine, of any seriousness, where such 'rationing' would be built into the therapy programme in advance of the treatment and *without knowing in advance* the outcome. The barely hidden controlling factor is money, the cost of the treatment.

Of course, the obvious response is that in private psychotherapy the ability to pay whistles the tune. In an attempt to deal with this difficulty in my own practice, I have for many years operated a sliding scale and have successfully worked with the most impoverished clients, university undergraduates and others. At the same time I have to recognise that I can only 'afford' a certain number of such clients. In reality, it has never been a problem and I cannot remember a client leaving, prematurely, complaining of the 'cost' of the therapy in money terms. However, there may well be a factor of self-deception in this statement! I would find it painful to accept that a client left prematurely as a result of literally not having the means to pay, but this may have happened and gone unrecognised. On the other hand, some may have left prematurely because they felt 'it was not worth it'. The phrase in itself is deeply ambiguous, and encoded within it are a number of discrete judgements and intentions. After all, it takes time and effort to pursue psychotherapy on a long-term weekly basis and the activity needs to be supported by powerful motivation, which includes the relationship with the therapist. I imagine there are plenty of people who would like to experience it but who 'cannot afford the fees or time'.

One of the most interesting books I have ever read about psychoanalysis, *Psychoanalysis: The Impossible Profession* by Janet Malcolm (1981), doesn't flinch from discussing money in the therapeutic relationship. She quotes Freda Fromm-Reichmann (1950) who in turn quotes Freud when he advised that:

> an analyst shouldn't be ashamed to charge substantial fees, that he should collect regularly and that he shouldn't take free patients, on the grounds that free treatment increases some of a neurotic's resistances. . . . The absence of the regulating effect offered by the payment of a fee to the doctor makes itself very painfully felt: the whole relationship is removed from the real world, and the patient is deprived of a strong motive for endeavouring to bring the treatment to an end.

Nothing could be more frank and revealing about the place of money in human transactions. Aaron Green (a fictitious name protecting the identity of the subject of Malcolm's book) speaks very frankly about money and the importance of it in his life as an analyst:

> Now, fees are a subject that I am very sensitive about, for a number of reasons. . . . I frankly want more money than I

have, and I am envious of analysts who are rich, yet I can't bring myself to do what's necessary to increase my income – that is, to beg for referrals. . . . So I have unfilled hours, and am bitter. . . . I have a patient whose analysis has all but revolved around the paying of fees. . . . he didn't pay me for eight months. Yes, eight months! And I allowed it to happen. . . . I consider it one of the most heroic things I have ever done as an analyst.

Rarely do I hear such comments from my colleagues in private practice and I applaud Aaron for his frankness.

I have suffered an unpaid fee. A young middle-class woman, classically neurotic and demanding in her hopeless search for sufficient attention from both men and women (none was ever enough), came to see me on the recommendation of a former client. She paid me for each attendance as it occurred but then did not turn up for a booked appointment. I waited to hear from her, in my usual manner. Time passed, not a word. So I sent her a brief formal reminder. No response. I then sent her another reminder and an account for the missed session. Nothing. I sent another account. Nothing. I would inform the reader she came from a very well-off background and had a well-paid job. The account was never settled. I can only surmise that I had possibly failed in meeting her apparent insatiable needs and so her revenge was to leave without notice or discussion, and to deprive me of my fee. She implicitly denied any value that I might have held in the relationship with her. Such is the way of narcissism. I wasn't worth anything! That was wounding because, of course, I do want to be worth something, and the payment of my fee, even after she had abandoned the relationship, would have supported my self-esteem. But I was punished.

Dorothy Rowe in the chapter 'The Private Meaning of Money' in her book *The Real Meaning of Money* (1997) discusses the relationship of money to self-esteem, status and male competition, and the tension that surrounds the secrets of income and fees and earnings of all kinds. She talks of the manner in which we hide from our colleagues our earnings although we may well discuss more 'personal' difficulties. For some years I served on the Governing Council of an English university and I remember 'putting my foot in it' (*shit*) when I asked the Vice Chancellor to tell us how much a newly appointed professor was going to be paid. The VC was astounded at my vulgar question and made it clear that the question was taboo. It was much too personal and intrusive and at the same time political. The chairman of the meeting hurriedly moved us forward to safer, cleaner business.

There is a somewhat darkly comic account concerning money, and the way it becomes the punishing issue between therapist and client, in Professor Stuart Sutherland's book *Breakdown* (1976). This centres around a client's account of a major psychological breakdown and his subsequent journey through therapy. Sutherland writes:

> I was so annoyed with him [the therapist] for what I regarded as very unhelpful treatment that I did not pay his bill. When many months later I received a peremptory letter from his solicitors, I took legal advice myself and wrote to him stating I had no intention of paying. I contested his claim on the grounds that his treatment had been incompetent.

Sutherland's angry and speedy legal response brought a placatory response from the therapist. I don't blame him! (the therapist I mean). In the same book, immediately after this account of conflict, Sutherland describes all his then anxiety and misfortunes with money and the handling of it. At one point he sold a second-hand car for as little as two pounds! He became convinced that he would lose his job and that his family would become destitute. He was in the grip of overwhelming anxiety much of which revolved around the meaning of money in his life and so it is not at all surprising that his therapist became entangled, drawn into the theatre of anxiety, symbolic loss and psychic mismanagement the client was suffering. However, we should remember the words of Liam Clarke: 'A double bind operates within psychoanalysis in that whatever one protests about, be it money charged . . . there exists a tendency to interpret such protests as camouflaging deeper motives' (1998).

Jeffrey Masson (1992), too, has written extensively on this tendency, and psychoanalysis is a form of relationship which can easily be manipulated in this way, to the frustration of the protesting client. As I write this I am conscious that my treatment of the subject of 'money' in psychotherapy, and its symbolic meaning, lends itself to the psychoanalytic trickery of deconstructing its vulgar reality and honesty in favour of a 'deeper' meaning where the social vulgarity would be hidden.

It disturbs me somewhat that those trainees who are trained in institutes that are firmly wedded to public health service or private hospital practice, see patients in an institutionalised context, where fees are negotiated in a bureaucratic manner and not within the therapeutic relationship. They are being very poorly prepared either to face the special conditions of private practice, which they may enter full or part-time, or to respond to the nature of the issues of gratification, reward and punishment and shame, which are so evidently present when money is brought into the equation (or even in its absence when therapy is supposedly 'free').

The late Nina Coltart devoted a couple of pages in her last book to the issue of money and although she wrote with disarming frankness concerning the importance of money to the therapist, there is an air of avoidance about the manner in which she describes and recommends the management of fees between client and therapist (Coltart, 1993). She was concerned that if by asking for cash the therapist might be seen as trying to avoid paying tax! Not an uncommon fantasy on the part of clients, in my experience, but surely a matter of therapeutic interest in the transference: the dishonest, fraudulent therapist = parent! She suggests that the money transaction is addressed immediately, in the earliest moments of therapy and I agree with her. But she is not too happy with the issue of cash. She preferred to ask for a cheque which is then paid to her in response to a bill, placed in an envelope hidden from view, on the consulting room table. Nevertheless she writes: 'A quantity of emotion of all sorts attaches to money, and the question of payment deserves fuller attention' (1993). I only wish she had gone a step further and perhaps discussed the intra-psychic, social and symbolic nature of money that she hints at in the introduction to the discussion.

To conclude, it is interesting to reflect briefly upon the matter of money in the life of Sigmund Freud. Ronald Clark in his biography of Freud touches on Freud's preoccupation with money and his constant struggle in the early days to earn enough to maintain a growing family:

his own position remained precarious. He never fell back to the near penury of his first days in practice; but keeping up the appearance of a successful doctor was still an effort that strained his resources, and he was grateful for financial aid from colleagues; still unable to pay back Breuer. (Clark, 1982)

The place of Breuer as an alter ego figure is well known and it is almost certainly true that Freud ended his days still in debt to him both emotionally and financially. I suppose it can be argued that we all end up in an unrecoverable debt to our fathers. Ernest Jones's biography of Freud (1982) speaks of him 'borrowing regularly from friends'. Breuer, however, was the principal donor. He often used to lend or give Freud 'a certain sum', and this, according to Jones, went on for many years. Freud himself, according to Jones, stated: 'It increases my self respect to see how much I am worth to anyone.' This is a rather smart way of describing the situation!

Rowe (1997) quotes a letter that Freud wrote to Fliess:

My mood depends very strongly on my earnings. Money is laughing gas for me. I know from my youth that once the wild horses of the pampas have been lassoed, they retain a certain anxiousness for life. Thus I have come to know the helplessness of poverty and continually fear it. You will see my style will improve and my ideas be more correct if this city provides me with an *ample livelihood*. (Rowe, 1997; my emphasis)

So the idea of value and personal worth is openly acknowledged by Freud, together with its inexorable link with money and relationships. I believe it behoves analytic psychotherapists in private practice to embrace the discussion of money and therapy boldly; not to feel too ashamed of the part money plays in our professional life but to look at our 'big jobs' without embarrassment and to recognise its importance in establishing a sense of worth in ourselves and our clients. As for our NHS colleagues (or any other therapists who receive salaries else where) they too should dwell for a while on the issues raised in this chapter and consider what they can do to strengthen their clients's position in the therapeutic relationship without losing out themselves.

Perhaps they should consider the idea that, instead of money from the client, what the therapist gets is a sense of power, which in itself is a dangerous currency.

As for those trainees working for 'nothing' for their training institutes, they too may benefit from giving these issues some attention. They should raise the matter of money, its meaning and place in the training relationship, with the training institutes and be prepared to face the consequences. And the best of luck!

5 Anxiety and Resistance in the Psychotherapeutic Relationship

> *The basic theory of client-centred therapy can be stated simply in the form of an 'if . . . then' hypothesis. If certain conditions are present in the attitudes of the person designated 'therapist' in a relationship, namely congruence, positive regard, and empathic understanding, then growthful change will take place in the 'other', the person designated 'client'.*
> (B. M. Meador and Carl R. Rogers, quoted in Corsini, 1973)

In earlier chapters I have touched briefly upon the idea of 'resistance'. In this chapter I shall expand on the subject looking closer and hopefully deeper into its presence and manifold manifestations especially in relation to the experience of anxiety. Many years ago when I was a student at university, our psychology lecturer stated: 'Worry is a useless reaction', and I copied this down in my notebook. Later, however, I began to think about it. Wasn't it evident that virtually all men and beasts 'worried'. So there must be a reason for this. It was functional, so how could it be useless? I never asked him and I wish now I had.

This morning I wake up feeling depressed, heavy, lacking in energy and interest, remembering reluctantly (resistance) that I have four clients to see today. Too many, I think (anxiety). Who are they? I strive to remember but strangely I can only bring one name to mind, Lawrence, a gay man. I find him entertaining and frustrating. When is he coming? Then I remember he is the first – I feel a bit better. Crawl out of bed, put on my dressing gown, wander into the bathroom, brush my teeth, refresh my mouth with mouthwash and go slowly down to breakfast. While reading the *Guardian* I have forgotten (resistance) about my busy day, and now my wife has to chivvy me along to get me back to the bathroom for my morning dip. I hate weak showers. In the bath quite suddenly the other names come to mind and I groan (resistance/anxiety). It is 'Misery Ann's' day and she comes first thing after lunch. What a hellish thought (anxiety). The day is just beginning and I am vacillating already. I need to address the 'hellish thought' and let Ann into my mind, even welcome her coming, for I know we are now, at last, working together and small but significant advances are being made. I need to recognise, too, that Lawrence, an easier 'cup of tea', remains elusive and playful, always slightly out of reach. I still have not given a thought to the other two clients coming this day. So what is the resistance doing to me? It is early and I long to abandon the struggle (resistance/anxiety).

To be or not to be? That is the question.
Shall I or shan't I.
Maybe I will or maybe I won't.
Perhaps I should.
Or should I?
Why should I?
I shan't!
I SHALL.

The above, although a roughly accurate account of real feelings, at a particular moment in my life as a therapist, is somewhat dramatised to enable me to make a point, which is that therapists as well as clients can feel resistant to work in psychotherapy and can experience varying levels of anxiety. It should be borne in mind that I work alone in a small private practice; I do not have the benefit of a relationship with colleagues, to whom I can unload, make a joke or have a moan; I have no employer to scapegoat for deficiencies in the 'set up'. I have only myself 'to blame', although my wife, as instanced above, provides powerful support. It is true that I can seek professional supervision.

Resistance can take many forms, and the indecisiveness, conflict and procrastination in the phrases given above are only an example of the more common problems we all struggle with, through our everyday lives. We do not always think of this as resistance but it often is. I went to a seminar recently where a well-known and distinguished counsellor/academic/author/ professor replied to a question I put to him concerning the manner in which person-centred counsellors might respond to resistance when encountering it with their clients. He stated quite frankly: 'We counsellors do not like resistance.' He said no more, perhaps implying a reluctance to admit to its presence in the counselling relationship. The audience, mostly trainee and experienced counsellors, sat in silence. Nothing more was said. I felt impatient. But what was to be expected? I was in the presence of mass resistance – even a degree of anxiety as their iconic hero was suddenly challenged.

Often resistance is no more than procrastination, known about but not addressed, as in the seminar. But sometimes it is much more sinister, amounting to a complete amnesiastic forgetting, when faced with a prompt to remember an incident or relationship. Sometimes even when the material is remembered the response is either to deny its presence or, more commonly, its significance. Sometimes we can actually collude with clients in their resistant manoeuvres. Then resistance moves into denial. Throughout the whole history of human relationships resistance has been experienced in interpersonal relationships in one form or another and to many varying levels of significance. Although Freud wrote about resistance (Freud, 1974) he did not discover it. Indeed, it could be said that all he did was to encounter it, and struggle with it as best he could in his clinical practice (see Jacobs, 1992). He found it in the lives of his clients and in his own partialities, as I found in mine, as recounted in my opening paragraph to this chapter, and as this following personal example also shows only too clearly.

Example

> *Attending a funeral at which I knew a number of my former colleagues would be present, I naturally looked for them at the crematorium. Most of the expected persons were present but there was one exception. This person was a man of professional standing, a person whom I had employed on a consultancy basis many years before and with whom at the time I had invested a great deal of trust. To cut a long story short I had asked him to carry out an important assignment for me and arranged to pay him a good fee for his anticipated services. He let me down and, after months of delay and procrastination on his part, I had to*

terminate the contract. I found this act very embarrassing at the time and was full of anxiety about the implications of such an act. I did not discuss his failure and my action with anyone else, and it felt like a stain on my professional life. I felt strangely guilty as if I had failed the commission. This was compounded by a failure on both our parts to discuss the issue and acknowledge the pain we were in. Anyway, it was only afterwards on my way home in the car I realised from conversations with other colleagues present, that he had been at the funeral and I had failed to recognise him in every sense of the word. He had not approached me and I had simply not 'seen' him. Consequently I had not recognised him with a gesture or word of greeting. He was without a doubt present at the crematorium and in the grounds outside, where those attending recognised and greeted old friends and colleagues. I subsequently wondered if he had 'recognised' me? My erstwhile colleagues were too tactful to mention any comment by him at my failure to see him. After all it was a funeral, and grievances should be put aside.

Freud (1973) wrote about resistance at length. The essence of his writing was that both in the unconscious mind and in the conscious (ego) self, resistance was to be encountered. He was especially concerned with its presence in the analytic relationship where it appeared as an impediment to analysis. However, we need to be aware that it is a part of the 'normal' everyday experience we have of ourselves in interpersonal and social relationships. Resistance in psychotherapy is usually seen as a defence. We defend ourselves against painful experiences and the memories of those experiences. We defend against anxiety. The defence against feelings of anxiety seems to reflect our capacity to manage anxious states within ourselves. The other factor in dealing with anxiety is to consider what happens when we cannot manage the anxiousness and it threatens our well being. It is threatening because the fundamental cause of the anxiety is not being addressed, rather it is often being repressed or suppressed. Consequently, the flood of anxious feeling simply occupies the psychic space, confusing the origins of the condition, sometimes replacing it with a false substitute. What are known as phobic states are a clear example of this mechanism in action. Malan (1979), consciously using psychiatric language, points out that 'reactive' anxiety is a different kind of creature to that which is deeply embedded in psychodynamic material. The problem is to know which is which, especially as the client may not be able to identify the difference for himself.

Example

James came to see me on the recommendation from a counsellor who had seen him for six sessions as part of an employee support service run by a big bank. His GP had described him as suffering from depression. He presented as a large, well-groomed and relaxed figure, cheerful of countenance and forthright in his opinions. For a 'depressed' man he cut a confident figure. I was somewhat surprised by all this when I first met him. A doctor had diagnosed his 'depression' after he came to the surgery asking for sleeping pills and describing sexual dysfunction. As he put it: 'I can't get it up.'

The doctor, a man, gave him a certificate for two weeks off from work, which he appeared to accept gladly, although describing himself as puzzled by the notion that he was depressed. He then spoke to me about his not wanting to go back to work and this puzzled him. He had, he said, a very good easy job. Basically he acted as mentor within the firm, going around 'making himself pleasant', as he said. He enjoyed this beneficent role and was well paid for doing it. The Personnel Department of the firm then referred him to a counselling service, contracted to the bank. They in turn referred him to a local counsellor who agreed to see him for six sessions. She did, and at the end of the six weeks confessed to me that she felt no wiser concerning his so-called depression then she had at the beginning of the relationship. She asked if I would see him. He would come as a private client at his own expense. I agreed.

What was so noticeable about James was that his life at that time was entirely driven by feelings – rationality and balance hardly came into it. When asked by his wife and relatives why he would not go back to work, he would only say he did not wish to do so. 'There is nothing more to say,' he would add firmly. He could give no rational explanation for his behaviour and, of course, his sexual dysfunction was not spoken about in his marriage. Again his wife was offered no explanation. He could only point to his wilting penis. At the same time he made strong declarations of love towards her.

After many weeks of therapy it became apparent that James had 'forgotten' much of his past and could not recall any feelings concerning early childhood relationships, especially with his mother. He could just remember his father being a quiet pleasant figure, not given to much self-expression. Being an only child he remembered feeling lonely sometimes and always wanting to please. Which he still did. But these general memories were about as much as he could recall. His past was bland, uninformed emotionally and muted in its remembered content and texture. He was in a special and highly effective state of memory denial, a kind of amnesia. The resistance was unwitting and located largely in his unconscious mind. Consciously, although very polite and conforming, he began to get annoyed with me for inviting him to remember material that he considered was all in the past, of no relevance to his current difficulties.

It was at this point that I began to experience the resistance weakening. Anger, barely concealed, flowed towards me. Even my most oblique or muted references to his childhood relationship with his mother produced feelings in him which, although he tried to conceal them leaked out as polite irritation. Similarly, any implied questioning of the depth or truth of his feelings for his wife produced denial. All he wanted to reveal was his sense of admiration for her. He praised her dealings with his two children and her forbearance in his failure to love her physically. He was deeply shocked when I attempted to get him to address his feelings towards his daughters and the absence of a son. He knew his wife would welcome another pregnancy, but as he put it with a smile on his face, without any apparent anxiety, 'Jolly decent of her. It would be good, but there you are, I can't get it up!' It was about this time that he suddenly made a confession. He fancied a young woman at work. A high flyer well thought of by her superiors. He liked virtually everything about her, especially the rather severe way she dressed in a just-above-the-knee-length black skirt, tights, white blouse, set off by a deep purple silk scarf and a black jacket. 'God, she's sexy. Wonderful shapely legs, gorgeous breasts and a really neat little bum,' he crooned. I put it to him bluntly, 'You would like to get her into bed.' I put this as a statement rather

*than a question. He flashed me a look. Man to man as it were.
'You bet.' But he made no move to seduce or even interest her in
himself; he simply relished the feeling of sexuality in himself,
which he thought long gone. His sexual potential had found a
home in fantasy about her body, at least parts of her body, and the
surface presentation of herself: assertive, assured and fertile.*

*This was obviously a turning point. No longer was there a
general declaration of sexual dysfunction. The problem was
firmly embedded in the intimacy of his marriage, with its roots
in the history of his relationships with women in close and controlling relationships with him. Soon he was recalling a mad fling at
university, with lots of sex, that petered out under his sterile petty
criticism. There had been an extramarital affair that had
lingered on for three years fuelled by the woman's refusal to allow
him to penetrate her, although 'petting' was allowed, up to the
point of orgasm by him, but not by her. Angry with her he found
it very difficult to admit an attraction to her that kept him
locked into a frustrating relationship with her. She finally
released him by taking up with a fellow she met in a garden
centre. The rural fecundity seemed to me appropriate. His
thoughts then turned to his mother. Gradually he began to allow
that relationship into therapy. She emerged and the censorship we
had experienced began to lift. The resistance was lifting. He felt
freer and I did too. Less anxious and consequently more able to
deal with his anxiety in a therapeutic manner.*

This example is interesting because it illustrates how effective,
and at the same time elusive, is the process of resistance. Much
has been written on the subject and it appears to be the belief of
some psychoanalytical psychotherapists working in a 'relational'
perspective (for example, Mitchell, 1995) that the therapist needs
to enter the deeply subjective world of the client. The need is to
share and understand the repressed material that is seeking expo-
sition and, at the same time, is being resisted through all sorts of
stratagems of both ego and id. To say this is easy, to accomplish
it is more difficult. It implies working with the resistance rather
than against it.

There is the long-standing danger of confusion and compromise in the therapeutic relationship to be addressed and dealt
with. Issues of transference will quickly become evident and these

are frequently immediate in character. I notice that some of my clients will attribute all kinds of mistaken beliefs and statements to me concerning their ongoing therapy, which I might be able to avoid more easily if I took up a remoter position in the therapeutic relationship. Usually these confusions simply produce rich material to be dealt with. I find that as long as I maintain that all transactions in the therapy room are bound within the therapeutic relationship, and that contract and boundaries both physically and emotionally are held within our respective roles, then no harm comes to either of us in the exchange. I suppose what becomes obvious is the risk attendant upon the practice of relational analytic psychotherapy as far as the therapist is concerned. I had a colleague say to me recently that, although he was gratified to see his private practice grow, he was becoming worried lest he find it all too much to cope with. He meant, clearly, that the coping was primarily emotional and he wasn't sure how much he could manage in terms of client numbers. His accommodation was secure, his financial situation was improving, his health was fine but he was becoming aware that increasing his client load was demanding more than just his time. He was beginning to experience resistance to his work and identity as an analytical psychotherapist. I could easily empathise with him. All psychotherapists struggle with these issues, preferably outside the consulting room. A growing awareness of anxiety in our work may act as an advance warning of other issues to follow, which need our attention. In the case of the 'overworked' therapist, the significant issue may well be the amount of emotional engagement he is capable of sustaining with those who are closest to him in his sexual and social life. Freud warned therapists that they may well be working on a level of personal deficit as the normal rewards of interpersonal gain are not met in the therapy room. It is commonly understood that for most people the place of work is a place of social and emotional gain. However, this is only partially true for psychotherapists, depending on the circumstances of their practice. The stand-alone therapist certainly needs to take this factor into account and heed the warning signs of anxiety if they begin to accrue.

As an alternative to this relational approach in therapy some other therapists and counsellors shelter behind a reflective, distant, unrevealing manner in the therapeutic situation. It is not for me to question their position. It is not mine as I have become steadily more convinced of the need for emotional engagement during my twenty years of experience in psychoanalytic psychotherapy. However, I sense I need to say more to clarify the situation for readers who are neither sympathetic towards, nor experienced in, what I am describing.

I would ask readers to look back to Chapter 1 where I describe a first encounter with a woman client I call Judith, where from the very first encounter in the therapy room a charged emotional atmosphere was present. I always try to react to such situations with curiosity when strong feeling, confusion, irritability or anxiety wells up in me. The aim is to allow the feeling into my conscious presence whilst at the same time examining the meaning of its presence. This is a tricky thing to do when the moments of exchange with a client may be coming thick and fast and there is little time for reflection. There are those who might say, 'Well, create time by holding back, creating a space of time, of silence in which to consider the situation.' Although this sounds fine and is sometimes an appropriate course of action, it can sometimes risk the loss of the emotional moment. My curiosity is more than simply attributing the feelings to counter-transference, it is nearer to examining the emotional realities of the moment as they emerge, and realising that the client is calling for an appropriate exchange.

Example

This was my response to Judith . . . and at a later stage of the therapy she admitted it had surprised her. She expected a distance from me, coolness supported by silence; the reflective mirror approach. This I can do and would if I thought that it was called for in the therapeutic situation. But with Judith I did not think it was a good way of responding to her powerful emotional demands at that moment. A small remembered example is of the occasion when she looked at me with barely repressed anger and pointed to a coffee table by my legs: 'Why do you put the coffee table there?' she demanded. 'It gets in the way, it gets between us!' She seemed to be demanding an emotional regime in her therapy and, if she received it, then she could use the experience to approach her anxious resistances, overcome them and proceed to work therapeutically. I was prepared to explore that avenue. My immediate response to her was challenging. I pretty bluntly asked her what use she could make of our relationship if we were actually physically closer. I asked her if she would really like to curl up on my lap. There was silence and she looked at the floor for what seemed an age. Her irritation disappeared. She looked up and gave a tentative smile and said, 'Well, I suppose that's what's missing, isn't it.' I nodded.

I was gratified when, after a couple of years of work together, as she was preparing to leave, she acknowledged how important my emotional involvement in the therapy had been. The point here was not that I had got involved in any collusive way with her, but rather that I had understood the feelings expressed and had been able to reply with a therapeutic emotional response; genuine, congruent (as Meador and Rogers, 1972, would say), helpful, unthreatening and ethical.

What is it that clients are fearful to reveal? Why the guilt, shame and accompanying anxiety? The *Pocket Oxford English Dictionary* has a neat definition for the word 'shame' which is both concise and accurate: 'distress or humiliation caused by consciousness of one's guilt, dishonour, or folly'. For 'guilt' it states: 'feeling of having done wrong'.

These states of mind seem to be universal and indeed an absence of them would tend to suggest psychopathy. Freud suggested that successful repression and the development of the super ego, a strong conscience, was the basis of civilisation. Those of this author's generation who recall or witnessed the absence of guilt displayed by groups of uniformed and armed men in the Second World War, will testify to the consequences of the absence of moral feelings that would inhibit torture, murder, mass slaughter and mayhem (see Levi, 1981). There was the destruction and murder of peasant peoples in Vietnam and the Far East during the 'hot period' of the Cold War, when thousands of tons of bombs fell upon them without discrimination, and chemical weapons were used without question. All this testifies to the manner in which perfectly decent people in aeroplanes can suspend their moral disgust as a response to orders from those in authority over them. After these events the airmen then have to 'forget' what they have done. The conditions of their actions, remote and visually distant, where the evidence of their actions is not immediately obvious, assist the process of forgetting and repressing. Sometimes this is a totally successful response but it should not surprise anyone that these airmen, at a much later stage of their lives, sometimes returned mentally to their atrocities, with intense anxiety and dismay. As I write there have been reports in the press of Israeli airmen refusing to bomb civilian targets in the Palestinian towns and refugee camps. The process of forgetting and repressing has failed. As moral anxiety exerts a telling influence authority is defied and civilised values are upheld.

In a recent book review in the *Guardian*, Elaine Showalter has an interesting commentary to make on the work of Pat Barker, the author of *Regeneration*, when she takes her to task for comparing herself to the psychoanalyst who she portrays as being 'totally involved but also totally detached . . . enabling you to take the hot coals out of the fire without being burned'. Showalter finds it difficult to believe that this is a tenable position to hold either as a writer or a therapist. I tend to agree and it worries me that some therapists, especially those in training, believe they can hold such a position of detachment, that they will never feel the hot coals. Nicholas Humphreys (2003) provides a vivid account of feeling the hot coals and managing the suffering of a painful encounter:

> A sudden fear about not knowing what to do seemed to complement her despairing statement that she felt she had lost her soul. My state of mind mirrored her description . . . my feeling [was] that I had lost a hold of myself, as if I were about to fall through the ice . . . seen to arise from her projective identification.

It always appears that projections towards us as therapists are most effective when we are prepared to receive them, and they become attached to feeling states that are genuinely held by the therapist.

For most of our clients the guilt they feel is not attached to obvious acts of barbarism. Indeed, for most of them their guilt lies in not only what they have done but also what they secretly wish to do or have failed to do. And most of these experiences, real or imagined, are associated with personal and social relationships, close and immediate, and are quite unlike the experience of bombing and killing people you do not know or wish to know. In the contemporary cult television series *The Sopranos*, one of the most intriguing features is the manner in which a Mafia boss, a family man, can kill without qualm, either directly or indirectly, those he sees as betraying or threatening him. In the next moment he is filled with guilt at forgetting to go to one of his children's school sports events. His wife attacks him for his forgetfulness and insensitivity and he wriggles with shame in the face of her righteous maternal anger. A neat paradox in this series is that he attends therapy with a psychoanalytic therapist, who becomes deeply embroiled with his state of denial and repression, in which his 'forgotten' feelings of shame and guilt fail to be addressed. So the therapist, too, is pushed into a position of denial and resistance, from which she fails to escape. She is, however, filled with feelings of anxiety that begin to undermine her professional position as a therapist. Perhaps the anxiety concerning her failing position as a therapist is a proper feeling. Maybe she will respond to the warning signals that are arising in her and she will react to correct the situation, thereby reclaiming her value as a psychotherapist. We wait to see if the scriptwriter will take her down that path or lead her further towards calamity.

Distress and humiliation are caused by consciousness of guilt, but it is arguable as to what degree of consciousness is required to instigate these feelings. The variety of human response to guilt and the consequent shame is infinitely variable. I recall a university English literature lecturer stating that T. S. Eliot said that 'human kind cannot bear very much reality'. But how much? That is the question. It appears that human beings are, by nature, remarkably secretive. Psychotherapy, in its training mode, stresses the need for revelation and openness, but as one who has received a good deal of training I was always aware of much that was not revealed. My rationalisations were endless and effective. I suspected that this was true, too, for many of my companion trainees. Indeed, I know it was true for at least one of them, who confessed as much to me in an 'outside group therapy' situation. He claimed a kind of pleasure at deceiving the therapist and the rest of the trainees. I, too, kept his secret for him! It seems that most of us have a capacity to conceal and to be highly selective about that which we reveal, even in the most secure situations, and at the same time to be aware of what we are doing.

However it seems that it is even more complicated than that. For example, it seems very likely that we can hold from our consciousness actions and thoughts that may bring about feelings of guilt. In this instance it may be an outside unexpected event that prompts us to remember actions and thoughts that we have been relatively successful in keeping from others and ourselves. At a more complicated level we may find that our conscious behaviour is a direct, if unconscious, reflection of that which we do not wish to know or be reminded. It is often claimed that psychoanalytical psychotherapy assists us in identifying and finding the strength to confront such material. It tends to claim its greatest success in uncovering the most deadly of interpersonal rivalries and destructive feelings that more often than not accrue in family situations. These feelings are frequently kept at bay and are not allowed much presence in the conscious mind, except perhaps as vague feelings of guilt when witnessing pain in other members of the family. The dynamics of projection, displacement and denial are complex but they play a powerful place in the process of resistance. Often to admit to full consciousness our most primitive feelings of love and hate is to court emotional and relational disaster.

The most obvious surface experience of what lies concealed in the unconscious is often unreasonable anxiety.

Example

> Mary, an attractive middle-aged social worker, came to me to enter into what she described as an adventure in finding out about herself. As usual I took her initial statement of intent with a degree of reserve, preferring a wait-and-see policy rather than one of immediate acceptance of her motives. She had an engaging and attractive family consisting of a husband and three sons. The husband was not an especially ambitious man but as a senior clerk in a big accountancy firm he made a decent living. Mary was more ambitious and she engaged in post-professional training at

every opportunity to improve her chances of promotion. The eldest son was away from home living independently in a southern town working as a teacher; he had a partner and seemed settled and happy. Another son lived at home but was attending local college training in IT skills. Another son lived nominally at home but spent a lot of time at his girlfriend's flat. He had no regular occupation but showed creative talent as an actor and singer and occasionally performed with small local groups at various gigs. However he refused to go to college on the grounds that it could teach him nothing. Mary was worried about him and resented his dependency whilst at the same time admiring his charisma and talents. As she said to me, 'He can get anything out of me. His father doesn't care and never lifts a finger.' A finger to do what? I wondered. This became a theme very early on in the therapy: the youngest son's blatant manipulation of his mother together with his father's apparent indifference to his behaviour kept coming into the therapy room in one form or another. One day Mary came into the therapy room for a morning appointment.

This was an unusual time but it proved productive. She literally fell into her usual chair in a somewhat dramatised gesture of exhaustion and exasperation. 'That boy, he will be the death of me. I must be a mass of bruises.' I said nothing and waited. 'Getting him out of bed before I leave the house is murder,' she continued. 'The lazy pig. I threw him out eventually. I cooked his breakfast and he was too damned lazy to come and get it. It makes me furious. It's the same every morning.' By now she was sitting up in her chair and adjusting her jacket, smoothing her hair and straightening her skirt. 'I must look a right mess.'

It was as if her relationship with this, the youngest son, was bursting out of its normal constraints. It was the first time he had been described to me in such emotional terms and with such excitement. I felt an unconscious truth was being allowed into the therapy space. The implied sexuality of the story and her obvious enjoyment of this morning ritual, slimly disguised as anxious exasperation, were patently obvious. I reminded her of her family of origin and said quietly that her remarks reminded me of stories she had told about her older brother when they tussled and struggled for the possession of the ball when playing on the beach. They both had been in their early teens, he the older. She had described with glee falling down in the sand, clutching the ball to her chest; her brother falling on top of her, tearing at her clenched fists in attempting to wrench it from her. She told me they were like puppies scrapping and playing, and she enjoyed the contact with him and knew he did with her too. Her mother, becoming uneasy at such horseplay, had eventually forbidden it, much to the annoyance of both brother and sister. Sex entered her mind.

She went on to describe her marriage as comfortable, companionate and sexless. She admitted that she deliberately created a fantasy life of sexual adventure with powerful demanding male figures in the foreground of her masturbatory images. She remembered with satisfaction her invention of a lover sensitively attentive to her sexual needs as well as being a vigorous lover. Gradually she began to admit that her playfulness with her son was a means of keeping him near to her, compensating for her husband's apathy and laziness. She admitted that the play had, as she put it, 'an edge to it' and that this sometimes worried her. She would then 'back off' only to return to the horseplay after an interval of a couple of weeks or so.

All this material fed into her anxieties as to what would happen when all the boys had left home. How would she survive emotionally, especially as her husband (some eight years older than her) was talking of early retirement. She was somewhat puzzled, too, at her husband's lazy indifference to the situation. He always balked at reprimanding his son for his lie-a-bed habits and made no comment on the laughing, giggly scenes he witnessed most mornings. Gradually the Oedipal scene unveiled itself, a scene that had been masked for many months of therapy, and the fuller implications of the situation began to impact on Mary. Accompanying it was a defensive anxiety screen that enabled her to 'put on hold', as she would cheerfully say, the 'problem of my marriage'.

Juliet Mitchell (1976) discusses recent academic views of the Oedipal complex and, although supporting contemporary criticism of Freud for being phallocentric in his approach to early male and female child development, she also acknowledges the importance of what is sometimes described as the Electra complex. The Electra complex (Feasey, 1982) is at least as important as the Oedipal complex in the experience of the women I have seen in my private practice (see also Owen, 1983). It is commonly held that many women find separation from their mothers very difficult. Indeed, the continuing presence of their mothers in terms of psychological attachment is evident to most observers. For the most part this attachment does not present pathologically in any significant way. However, the emotional link with the mother does not usually reach the point of abandonment, as the feminine destiny (procreation) provides a powerful drive towards the maintenance of the mother/daughter alliance. However, most young women apparently need a transitory period of erotic love for their fathers to accomplish their maturation as sexual individuals, capable of living autonomously and, eventually, achieving physical love with another man. If this is not achieved, and the girl remains locked into a deeply attached relationship with her mother, then problems may arise in the process of achieving a successful sexual life. The intrusive third voice of an imagined or real critical mother resisting separation has to be faced and struggled with. It is often at this point that women desperately seek their absent father, or look for a substitute fatherly relationship in order to hold the mother at bay.

This scenario is usually accompanied by powerful anxiety which may be displaced onto less identifiable figures. The guilt, and consequent shame, that is sometimes associated when these problems arise, where the client discovers feelings of this character surfacing in moments of emotional distress, gives rise to resistance – resistance to the implications of the feelings, and anxiety that disclosure would be morally reprehensible. Hence some sort of neurotic displacement is common whereby the feelings get reinterpreted and expressed in what at first seems acceptable action. However, this manoeuvre often fails and the client realises he or she needs professional help in dealing with the situation.

In the example quoted above it was the absence of her husband from the sexual scene, his easily contrived blindness or indifference to the horseplay he witnessed, that spurred on both wife (mother) and son to the slightly hazardous game they were playing with each other. Mary was angry, waiting for her lazy husband to act, to intervene, to push his son out of the nest and tell him to find one of his own. She wanted his sexual attention too, wanted their easy companionate relationship transformed into the attraction that had once been shared between them. She knew she was an attractive woman. So why was he indifferent to her sexual presence? The son, too, was waiting to be disillusioned, to be released from his mother's sexual energy and charm so that he could eat his breakfast in the silence of filial indifference and distance, looking for entertainment and fulfilment elsewhere. And, perhaps, finding true feelings towards his father. If her aims could be achieved, then the family anxiety level, however displayed, would be eased and all would benefit from a more harmonious and fulfilling emotional milieu.

Luepnitz (2003) sums up the therapeutic task well (applied both to the therapist/client relationship and to our many personal relationships around us) when she says: 'To choose solitude freely, to love and engage fully – both are capacities to be desired. Herein lies the work of the talking cure.'

6 A Suitable Case for Treatment*

It is all very well using a sub-title like 'Intimacy Between Strangers' where the unthinking assumption might well be that a 'stranger' is merely someone rather like oneself, who we have not met before, who in therapy will connect with us as therapists on relatively common ground. But in contemporary Britain this casual assumption cannot be made with any great certainty. The truth is that our 'stranger' may come from a background of social, cultural, religious, ethnic, class, national identity and sexual orientation with which we are completely out of touch. The first telephone call may betray difference but sometimes it is not until the doorstep meeting that the stranger is really revealed as 'strange'.

I want to consider in this chapter how some clients are judged suitable or otherwise for analytic psychotherapy. Historically, much thought has been given to the subject and a number of propositions have been put forward on the qualities to be looked for in a patient being proposed for psychoanalysis. Analytical psychotherapy and the more elusively titled psychodynamic psychotherapy are inheritors of this rather academic discussion. It usually arises in the training situation when trainees are advised to find a client suitable for the 'talking therapy'. They are often warned off unsuitable cases and not infrequently this becomes a matter of dispute involving trainees, training therapists and supervisors. Such descriptions as borderline personalities/schizoid personalities/personality disorders/cultural dissonance/concrete thinking, are used to express the reservation of the training and supervision staff who seek to steer trainees away from difficult or what could be regarded as unsuitable patients. Surrounding this debate are murky issues of class, race, ethnicity, culture, education, gender and sexual identification. I want to examine the idea of the unsuitable client and illustrate some of my own dilemmas

---

* An earlier version of this chapter originally appeared in *Changes Journal*, 16:2.

and experiences in relation to one particular client, and a few non-particular ones where I feel I have suffered some disadvantage and gained much valuable knowledge, but where the question of suitability might well have arisen.

I first became interested in this issue when a young highly intelligent trainee, Alan, came to me for supervision. He had became something of a problem for his tutors on the analytical psychotherapy training course – albeit an intellectual problem. He had been in dispute with the training committee concerning the choice of training client, in such a way that his training therapist had been sucked into the argument within the committee. The boundaries had became confused. I was asked to become the trainee's clinical supervisor to clarify the situation, and I agreed. I certainly regarded the disputed chosen patient as a challenge and I was willing to acknowledge the concern of the committee. However, looking back to my own experience as a trainee, and as a training supervisor, I felt the patient, given sufficient personal motivation, was workable with. I also thought Alan looked as if he would cope well with any difficulties that may arise And so it proved to be. This experience focussed my mind on the issue of suitability when assessing and selecting clients.

It is generally known that Sigmund Freud's patients, the subjects of his case studies were on the whole female and without exception middle class. Some of them were very intelligent and well educated, and a number of them in the latter period of his practice were would-be analysts seeking a training therapy. In most cases they were from a professional background. Freud himself did not seem to think it of any significance or interest that these were middle-class patients, many of them sharing a common class and cultural background. Certainly, he does not write about them in those terms. In his 'Introductory Lectures in Psychoanalysis' (1973) Freud consistently described his patients in the most generalised of terms, employing the adjective 'neurotic' to distinguish them from those he described as 'normal'. The subject of class hardly seems to have entered his consideration. This does not surprise me. Even today one can hardly imagine many psychoanalysts giving much consideration to the issue of class in their experience of private practice.

Geoffrey Gorer (1966), a social anthropologist, in a sharp and incisive essay in *Psychoanalysis Observed* comments with barely concealed irritation on the absence of 'cultural' understanding in the theories and practice of many twentieth-century psychoanalysts. He is particularly scathing of Melanie Klein, the founder of what is sometimes described as the 'British School'. It would appear that the notion of a patient having a valid or influential cultural experience upon which to draw as a contribution towards the therapy is of no significance or importance. Then there is the matter of the cost of private psychoanalytic therapy, placing it usually well beyond the means of working-class people, thereby excluding this socio-cultural group on economic groups. For analytic psychotherapists working in the public sector of mental health, however, it is a quite different story, and I feel sure for many of them it will be a significant question, to be resolved, one hopes, in favour of the patient.

Freud, however, was interested in what he described as 'external resistances' and he gives the subject some attention in his lecture mentioned above. He writes: 'many attempts at treatment miscarried during the early period of analysis because they . . . were undertaken in cases which were unsuited to our procedure and which we should exclude today'. In this instance he does not identify what he considers 'unsuitable' characteristics in a patient, but he does go on to describe what he calls 'unfavourable external conditions'. In this example, he is referring to the family of a patient who 'stick their noses into the field of operation', and he goes on to ask 'how can one ward off these external resistances?' He is very pessimistic about the possibility of successfully dealing with this situation and goes on to quote a case where a husband intervened and looked on the analytic procedure with 'disfavour' because he realised his 'own catalogue of sins will be brought to light'. In the light of what I have just presented of Freud's thinking, I should in all fairness quote him, again from the same source, where he writes: 'You will guess, of course, how much the prospect of treatment are determined by the patient's social milieu and the cultural level of his family.' Here I think Freud is using the term 'cultural' in an evaluative sense, not in the more modern sociological sense. What Freud describes as the social milieu and cultural level would probably now be interpreted as characteristic of class and education. At this point I wish to bring into focus another objection which Freud mentions and which is generally accepted in psychiatry as being contra-indicative for psychotherapy. Patients suffering from acute psychotic delusions are generally felt to be unsuitable for analytic psychotherapy because they cannot exercise 'insight' into their delusional system. Anthony Storr, whose work I shall be considering later on in this chapter, states on the issue of patients suffering from delusional paranoia and other psychotic problems, that 'they should not be treated by the beginner psychotherapist' (Storr, 1979). It is difficult to argue with this view but it speaks more of the limitations of the therapist than the unsuitability of the client!

This issue of suitability comes up again quite forcefully in the book *Individual Theory in Britain*, edited by Windy Dryden (1984) and a number of articles refer to selection as a problem and an area where the therapist needs to show skill in predicting likely outcomes. Dryden himself in the introductory chapter of the book discusses contributors such as Fay Fransella and Francesca Inskipp who write about the issue of over-dependency in potential clients. Dryden refers to Mackay who worries about the threat of intimacy to some clients when drawn into the closeness of a dyadic relationship with the therapist. Dryden cites Faye Page who believes that 'highly manipulative' patients may do better in groups than in the closer relationship offered in individual work, describing such patients as 'border-line patients'. The list continues: there are those who over-intellectualise, then there are those with sex problems which may contra-indicate for individual therapy. Finally, according to some contributors to the book, there are those highly skilful clients who find the individual therapeutic relationship too 'comfortable'. This reminds me of an occasion when working in Hungary I was asked by the director of a residential community therapy centre how I had fared with a staff workshop. When I replied that I had found the analytical staff the most difficult to work with, he replied blandly: 'Of course, they are the most experienced in defence'. They were probably 'too comfortable for their own good'. But aren't we all! And this includes the readers of this chapter.

Reading the list of reservations in Dryden's book, one begins to wonder who are the right people to become clients? One cannot help wondering if, as a profession, psychotherapists put their own conceptualisation of the 'right kind' of client before almost everything else in their thinking when selecting clients. One of the contributors to the book, Cassie Cooper, puts this forward quite clearly when she writes: 'The Kleinian therapist would see himself as working best with a patient whose underlying conflicts were towards the narcissistic side; whose ego had undergone considerable deformation or weakening.' Thus we see potential patients being classified into specific limited qualifying categories, following almost a medical model of specialised need and consequent treatment by specialist consultants. One can almost imagine a situation where such a categorisation could lead to the following fantasy scenario:

> Having had my narcissistic wounds treated by a clever Kleinian, and thankfully they are healed, I can now pay attention to my defective super ego. So I will seek a referral in that direction. A Freudian of the independent school should do the trick! I think I might finish off with some person-centred counselling to confirm my self esteem.

However, there is also a much broader category of patients who may be disallowed – those who are described as only capable of 'concrete thinking' and who attempt to resolve problems through action. They are said to 'act out', but to my mind this is a simplistic division as all of us to some extent or another, depending upon the particular circumstances of our lives, 'act out' and/or reflect with insight upon our dilemma, what ever that might be. Usually we have to 'act' in some way or another to bring about change. Our reflection on the process and consequent 'insight' might guide us in the right healthy direction or, as Foulkes (1957) puts it, 'into a state of equilibrium', or it might not. I do not believe that therapists are in any special privileged position in this respect. We have to approach with caution the notion of persons who think concretely and act, rather than reflect, as being unsuitable for psychotherapy. These persons are usually identified as working class in origin, of low educational attainment and regarded as not likely to exercise reflection and insight in the conduct of their lives. Can it be that this division, often employed in selecting patients for psychotherapy, is as reliable as we would wish it to be? I wish to introduce here a figure from my case studies.

Example

Sue is the daughter of a skilled working-class man of limited education. Her mother came from the same background but conducted herself in a more sophisticated manner. There was one other daughter just leaving school who also had had a period in psychiatric care. Sue came to me because she was said to be suffering from depression and this was giving rise to alarming experiences in her life, the greater part of which related to her boyfriend. She had had an abortion some five months earlier and she was complaining that her boyfriend treated her with contempt, verbally abusing her in front of their mutual friends. I suggested the family came to see me and somewhat to my surprise they agreed to the meeting. She claimed to feel nothing, and in the early sessions with her family she curled up in a large chair and groomed her hair with her fingers, in the manner of a cat looking for fleas, rarely saying anything. The attitude of the family towards her was one of irritation. Her mother was annoyed because Sue refused to take any drug treatment or to act in any way to relieve her situation. The family identified her as the 'patient'. My view was that I was dealing with a dysfunctional family. The principle instance of 'acting out', in the case of Sue, was the manner in which she invited her boyfriend to abuse and denigrate her socially. She was well aware of this situation and she could predict the behaviour that would drive him into abusive attitudes and actions, some of which was done in public in front of their mutual friends.

Yet she appeared quite unable to inhibit her provocations. She excited sadistic impulses in him and responded masochistically to his attacks on her. As far as the abortion was concerned she turned her natural wish to grieve to a pathological desire for punishment. This was experienced in a number of ways:

1. the loss of her usual friendly and extrovert manner;
2. the loss of her independence when she returned home to her mother;
3. the loss of her former loving and sexually fulfilling boyfriend, drawing from him a sadistic response and much sexual abuse in unloving sexual intercourse;

4. *the gradual loss of girlfriends who turned away from her drab and unshifting depression in disgust;*
5. *the loss of her relationship with her younger sister, who accused her of being attention-seeking and stupid.*

The only person who appeared to be prepared to stick by her was her father, and the Oedipal aspects of their relationship appeared to be quite obvious, especially as he was at the time thinking of leaving his wife. Of course, not everything can be attributed to the abortion. The fact of the matter is that she came from a dysfunctional family and she was not equipped with sufficient emotional strength or understanding to shape her own destiny. Quite the contrary. The family had never been securely underpinned with unworried love, common sense or insight. Rather, there had been a series of family crises that had been dealt with by impulsive actions in attempts to resolve challenging issues. The abortion and the subsequent depressive illness besetting Sue was merely the latest one.

My decision as a therapist faced with this family situation was to help them face the splitting that was just about to occur as the father left the family as a precursor to divorcing his wife. At the same time the youngest daughter left home. The family house was sold and enough capital went to the wife to provide her with another, more modest house. Sue went to live with her, although expressing a desire to live with her father. He, however, was soon to leave the country. In this situation it came as no surprise that Sue identified herself as the patient and asked me for psychotherapy.

At this point I would like to consider some of the criteria used by psychotherapists in selecting a patient for analytic psychotherapeutic treatment.

I have always found Anthony Storr's book *The Art of Psychotherapy* (1979) a most insightful and practical guide to the practice of therapy and he gives much attention to the character of patients who are referred for analytical psychotherapy. He discusses, for example, the patient who is reluctant to talk: 'This may be because of lack of education; a difficulty which is usually surmounted if the psychotherapist is flexible enough to adapt his use of language to the patient's range.' This is sound enough advice but the use of language is more subtle than Storr suggests in this discussion, and the therapist as well as the patient uses language coloured with values and class assumptions to convey both conscious and unconscious ideas and images of family and personality. Nevertheless I approve of Storr's optimism in believing that what in Britain are fundamentally class and racial elements, found in both therapist and patient, can be addressed and overcome in favour of the talking therapy. But it takes a great deal of consciousness and effort.

Writing from within an NHS context, Storr speaks about the group of patients who very rarely ever get a chance to talk to a psychotherapist. He describes them as: 'patients [who] have been brought up in such a way that they habitually have recourse to action, when faced with difficulties, and do not include putting things into words as a form of action'. He describes patients who get solace from drink, change their jobs, dig the garden furiously to alleviate anxiety – they wish to 'do something', however futile or inappropriate. He writes that 'It takes time to learn that clarification through words can be of use.' Storr recognises the difficulties of working dynamically with such patients, and states that: 'Some people also believe that any form of self-examination is to be deplored; that introspection is unhealthy and talking about one's problems self indulgent.'

This has been my experience. too, with some of the patients in my private practice. Some times these feelings are described by patients as vaguely understood moral injunctions not to be weak and they feel they should 'pull themselves together'. This can come from the puritanical inheritance of our white Anglo-Saxon Christian culture, where suffering and torment are sometimes described as purifying processes. On other occasions it is located in a class or race culture which decries the value of recognising and expressing feelings in a direct way. On yet other occasions it arises from the social psychology of a particular family where the patient has been actively discouraged from the revelation of feelings and when 'bad news' is not allowed, resulting in repression and 'acting' without insight. Whatever the cause, the situation brings great discomfort to the analytic psychotherapist, who sometimes describe these patients as being 'unsuitable' or beyond the reach of psychotherapy.

Example (continued)

> *As far as Sue was concerned, she 'acted out' inside the family by neglecting her appearance, by masochistically inviting and accepting derision, by refusing to help her mother in the house, by sleeping late and staying out, sometimes all night, without consultation with her mother. But her 'acting out' contained a powerful message that could not be ignored. It certainly drew attention to her condition and her suffering.*

Storr draws attention to the need for psychotherapy patients to take the lead in the process of therapy where, consequently, the therapist follows. This too implies a judgement in the assessment process as to how capable the patient is in providing this lead and in the manner of doing so.

Example (continued)

> *To refer back to Sue, when she was in the family therapy situation she gave no verbal leads but she did prompt me to pay attention to her by the way she used body language. As mentioned before, I noticed that when her mother spoke she simply avoided looking at her and would start picking away at pieces of skin on her hands as if she found her mother an irritation, a bore. She paid quite strong attention to her sister but her most obvious body gestures were towards her father. When he spoke she stared at him intensely, she twisted her body around to look at him and generally appeared to be interested in a guarded sort of way. So she 'acted' rather than spoke, but her intentions were clear enough. As the old saying goes, 'Action speaks louder than words.' In both the individual session as well as in the group, such gestures might well invite an interpretation and I would argue that all these acts, albeit from an unconscious level, are intended for the therapist to see and perhaps comment upon. So 'taking the lead' may well represent itself in a number of ways.*
>
> *I was not at all surprised that Sue referred herself to me for individual therapy and in the early sessions she learned to tolerate silence and to recognise that I would wait for her to begin the*

conversation, and that it didn't matter at what point she began. Here I am dealing with an intelligent, if uneducated, patient, but when she came to me she was deeply entrenched into a position of not admitting to any feeling and refusing to talk; there was a denial of intelligence and understanding. But she knew before she came she would talk, and that was the point of coming to see me.

This takes me onto another issue: the willingness that underpins all successful therapy. Sometimes clients are sent for therapy. I have experienced this mostly with adolescents. Parents in a desperate attempt to solve a problem sometimes send their young son or daughter for therapy. This forced situation needs to be addressed at an early stage. If the patient is not committed to therapy, and invests no special interest or hope in it, the outcome is unlikely to be positive. It is not so much that the patient is unsuitable but rather an unsuitable referral has been made on the part of parents unable to cope with a developing crisis. Here I have spoken of private referrals, but clients also come to me through doctors or social workers, often in such a way as to suggest that 'all else has failed so let's try psychotherapy!' Sue was not sent to me, she chose me as a result of coming with her family for some brief family therapy sessions. She chose to come by herself voluntarily and consequently I was reassured concerning her motivation. She had identified herself as being 'suitably' in need and me as a 'suitable' therapist.

Barbara Fletcham Smith in an informative and interesting article, 'Assessing the Difficulties for British Patients of Caribbean Origin on Being Referred for Psychoanalytic Psychotherapy' (1993), speaks of the difficulty a young woman of West Indian background had

in presenting herself as a suitable patient for psychotherapy, where her thoughts in the session were often muddled, forgotten or impossible to put into words [in a] talking therapy, in an environment in which such treatment was in short supply. (Smith, 1993)

In the same article she states:

Another point worth remembering is that there is some evidence that patients of Caribbean origin often come to the attention of the mental health services only when they are in the acute stage of mental illness, at which point they are admitted to hospital.

The inference here is that they have passed the stage of mental illness when they might have been identified as suitable for psychotherapy. Although I have no statistical proof, my twelve years working in a large psychiatric hospital leads me to believe that this is also true for many white working-class patients of Anglo-Saxon or European origin.

I had some personal experience of the crossing of ethnic and religious barriers when I was in hospital for a short time on a public ward. The man in the next bed, an immigrant from the Indian sub-continent, had been admitted following a stab wound to his chest, inflicted by a teenage daughter after a fierce quarrel concerning her dress and social behaviour. Relatives poured in to see him and there was much angry discussion around the bed as to what to do about the offending daughter. Eventually the ward sister chased them away to give the poor man a chance to rest and recover. Some hours later he began to talk to me. His misery and anxiety were manifest and I felt the best thing to do was to attempt to get him to tell me about his relationship with the daughter. I adopted a neutral but sympathetic manner, much in the manner I adopt in the consulting room. The discussion went on for about an hour and concluded with him realising and accepting that he was probably loved and admired by his daughter, and that feeling between them ran very deep. It was probable that she would now be racked with the emotional pain of guilt and anxiety. I was about twenty years older than this man, and I obviously appeared to him like an older wiser male, and he as good as said this to my wife. A positive transference had taken place. A couple of days later the daughter visited him and there was an attempt (albeit a difficult one) at reconciliation which, in part, was successful.

His wife was introduced to me and she took the opportunity to express her thanks for what she saw as a healing episode for her husband and daughter. My view was that only a start had been made and that much remained to be done. Nevertheless this man, once given the opportunity to talk about his feelings for his daughter and hers for him, seized eagerly upon the experience. In some good part his race and culture took second place to this therapeutic exchange. I do not wish to dismiss their importance here, and indeed sometimes their presence is critical. To be frank, I was surprised how cultural distance was overcome between us, our different skin colour and dress appearance dwindling in significance, as we seriously discussed this near family tragedy.

To return to Storr and to inverse his recommendations to the therapist, I suggest that when we assess suitability for analytic therapy we try to keep the following injunctions in mind:

1. the willingness and ability of the patient to take the lead, when it is made clear that is what is expected of them;
2. the willingness of the patient to take responsibility for helping themselves;
3. a willingness to co-operate with the therapist;
4. a willingness to try to find words to describe feeling states and to communicate with the therapist;
5. a willingness to come regularly and for some duration to therapy sessions as a product of informed choice.

Sue appeared to be able to meet all these criteria and to find the money to pay my fees, which, whilst not being extortionate (linked as they are to the patient's ability to pay), nevertheless do require payment.

Even in the terminal stages of a physical illness psychotherapy can have a part to play in the relief of pain and anxiety. In an interesting article in the journal *Psychoanalytic Psychotherapy*, Lawrence Goldie writes:

> Obviously there are those who cannot see the point of talking when it seems to have nothing to offer by way of pain relief or physical cure. In any event most patients have no experience or knowledge of psychotherapy. (Goldie, 1989)

However, when psychotherapy is offered and taken up, he writes: 'There is an impressive pacing, so that understanding is acquired rapidly once a worthwhile and interesting exchange occurs.' He then goes on: 'The naïveté of patients with regard to psychological treatment and mental processes is an advantage – instead of prejudice, there is exploratory interest.'

Example

This puts me in mind of a patient I had very early on in my career as a therapist, who I shall call Liz. She came from a working-class background and was a student studying sciences in my local university. She was promiscuous in a pathological way. She often hitchhiked and boasted to me of the sexual conquests she made among the drivers who picked her up. The beginning of insight for her was when she was ruminating in a very depressed way about the separation from her father, after her mother died of cancer, when she was about seven years old. She remembered being with her older brother (he was about ten years old) and standing in front of father who said: 'The first one to put his hand up stays with me!'

Before the sentence was complete her brother had thrust his hand into the air: he won! Liz remembered being full of jealous rage at what she saw as unfairness and rejection on the part of her father and triumph on the part of her brother. Despair filled her being as she grieved for the loss of her mother and the painful scenes of dying that she had witnessed, as her mother met death in the family home. Now she was to lose her father. He was rejecting her. From this memory came a string of other associations and memories. Furthermore, she began to see that a lot of her seductive behaviour towards me, and other men, was linked with that episode. Once her curiosity was aroused the therapy moved ahead productively, or as Goldie would say, 'an interesting exchange occurred'.

The late Nina Coltart is rather more demanding in her description of the factors looked for in the assessment interview. In her handbook *How to Survive as a Psychotherapist* (1993), she writes that a prospective patient should be able to demonstrate 'An acknowledgement that he has an unconscious life that affects thoughts and behaviour'. She goes on to say that prospective patients should:

- be able to give a self-aware history;
- show capacity to give this history without the prompting of the assessor;
- show the capacity to recall memories, with their appropriate affect;
- show some capacity to step back from his own story and to reflect upon it;
- show willingness to take responsibility for himself.

(Coltart, 1993)

The patient, furthermore, must use imagination combined with evidence of realistic self-esteem and a sense of the significance of the relationship with the assessor. Coltart is discussing here the idea of psychological mindedness which she sees as a prime factor in the selection of a suitable patient. However, it is my view that many of these qualities are not revealed until the unsuitable patient is actually engaged in therapy. Learning then takes place. This was certainly the case with Liz and to a large extent with Sue. In this sense psychotherapy emerges as an educational experience for the client.

David Malan in his book *Individual Psychotherapy and the Science of Psychodynamics* (1979) devotes several chapters to the question of assessment of patients for psychotherapy and the identification of the appropriate therapy for particular patients. Interestingly, however, he devotes little of the text to the characteristics of the patients themselves or their preferences. He is concerned instead with the position of the therapist and his/her skill in formulating the correct questions and interpretations in deciding which form of psychotherapy is the appropriate treatment for a particular patient. Medicine rules OK! He makes many valuable points in his discussion of the necessity for skilful and sensitive initial assessments with new potential patients and he seems insistent upon the therapist being able to make a formulation which is in good part predictive of outcome. He writes:

The interviewer's basic aim has already been stated and is simple enough, namely to obtain sufficient evidence to enable him to prescribe an appropriate intervention. . . . He needs to be able to forecast the kinds of events that are likely to occur as the patient interacts with a therapist and begins to face disturbing feelings. (Malan, 1979)

The proportion of discussion given to the requirements of the therapist as opposed to those of the patient shows a point of view that is heavily one-sided in its scrutiny of the intrinsic power relationship between doctor and patient. Implied in the section I have quoted is the inevitability of certain patient responses if a certain kind of therapy is offered. Here the idea of a dynamic learning environment is simply ignored.

To be fair to David Malan, he does favourably quote the work of Leonard Zegan, at Yale University, who advocates the training of people from socially deprived backgrounds in how to become psychotherapeutic patients. On the other hand, the essentially patronising position of such a suggestion seems to pass him by. Psychoanalysis has much to say about fathers!

More to my liking is the advice given by Joel Kovel in his invaluable book *A Complete Guide to Therapy* (1978). Here, he writes in response to the question 'What kind of person might benefit from psychotherapy?'

Generally speaking one with some verbal capacity, the ability to form relationships and to conduct something of a settled life. More essential perhaps is a genuine curiosity about oneself and the ability to tolerate frustration especially the painful non-gratification of transference feelings. If unambiguous and rapid answers are demanded of life, this is not a recommended form of treatment. (Kovel, 1978)

In general I find this statement reasonably satisfying and in favour of the 'unsuitable' client, despite its predictive character, whereas I find the Coltart statement of requirements slanted towards the needs of the therapist. This bias towards the therapist is all too often the situation in the assessment process and, in my view, needs addressing.

Somewhere in the middle stand Brown and Peddar in their

book *Introduction to Psychotherapy* (1979), where they devote a chapter to discussing selection and outcome. The opening page brings to the fore their concern with a potential patient being able to make appropriate responses to 'interpretation' and 'transference' as phenomena within the therapeutic relationship. It is obviously gratifying if a client intuitively responds to such prompting at an initial interview. On the other hand, when I think of some of the most gratifying cases I have worked with, it would be true to say that this kind of recognition and response has only come as the therapeutic relationship has proceeded and grown. And this takes time.

To conclude I would like to stress the need to treat the notion of the unsuitable client/patient with some caution. As David Pilgrim has pointed out in a powerful article in *Changes Journal* (Pilgrim, 1997), the practice of psychoanalytic psychotherapy can all too easily appear exclusive and elitist, too much bound up with its own definitions of reality, too much entrapped in its own exclusive, often reductionist, language. In my view his article is more a rhetorical cry of ideological pain then a considered critique of contemporary analytical psychotherapy. Nevertheless, his energetic and sometimes brilliant exposure of the failure of analytical thinking to confront and address the meaning of social experience, with its frequent abusive consequences, is quite evidently true – at least in my experience. Towards the end of his article, having loosed off his very considerable guns at the 'therapist journalists', he then starts to take a more 'balanced' view of his own arguments. However it is at this point that he weakens and falls back upon calls for 'outcome research' and the 'collective feedback of service users'. When the complexity of these proposals are faced I fear we shall end up with another set of categorisations concerning the validity of psychotherapy and its application to user groups. The 'Catch 22' of the situation is that those who do the interpretation of 'outcome research' and 'service user feedback' have their own cultural agenda and their own ideology. They have their own language and value systems just like the psychoanalysts. David Pilgrim should remember the famous quote from Heller's *Catch-22*: 'You can only get out of flying dangerous missions by being found "mad". BUT you have to be "mad" to fly.'

By inference Pilgrim supports my view that the notion of

unsuitability can easily be found to be unhappily judgemental in terms of class, race, gender, and what might be described as social and cultural practices (especially in the area of language), social rituals and behaviour. In an increasingly cosmopolitan United Kingdom there is an obvious need for psychotherapists to look at the accepted practices of the past to judge and amend them, as necessary, to meet the contemporary therapeutic needs of the population. As Pilgrim states: 'If psychotherapy is effective (and overall it appears to be, compared to no treatment) then it raises issues about equality of access.' That means availability to all social and cultural groups without discrimination and by choice.

Choice is a tricky matter. Choice is a matter of knowledge. How many NHS patients have unquestioningly swallowed the tablets because they had no knowledge of any alternative, or if they did, how to access it? If psychotherapy is a known option then a client may well shop around for a private psychotherapist and have a number of interviews; this is not an uncommon practice. However, when a patient is referred to a psychotherapy centre in the NHS for treatment, how much patient choice is then in evidence? Not much I would guess. Malan in his chapters on assessment for psychotherapy does not mention patient choice at all although he gives some space to 'resistance' and how to deal with it psychodynamically! Most of the time in Malan's assumptions there is the belief that the patient has no means of knowing, in an active intelligent way, whether psychotherapy will be useful or whether this particular therapist is the right one to work with.

We should constantly keep in mind that when Freud was writing, it was in the context of life in nineteenth-century central Europe, and he was responding, largely, to the needs of that time and place. Times have changed. Our clients are more sophisticated and better informed, perhaps as a result of reading Pilgrim's hated journalists! Perhaps we, as therapists, need to change too and should be less fearful of revisionism than we appear to be at present. Most of us as therapists have given serious attention to our intra-psychic world. Now, I believe, we need to allow our personal social construct to take its place in our professional considerations of our suitability to be therapists.

7 Remembering and Forgetting

A friend, half my age, said to me some time ago that he would be a useless client because he could remember so little about his childhood. My wife and I met up recently for a meal with my friend, his mother and father, and his partner. We were talking about his partner's small son, aged 9, and he said teasingly to her that soon the boy would stop adoring her and glimmers of hate would appear. I listened with interest to this and said nothing. The man's mother vehemently denied his forecast but his partner remained silent. He suddenly turned to his mother and said:

> Well, I can remember, mum, when I was about ten feeling hatred towards you when you chivvied Dad for wasting his time in front of rubbish television, wrestling, on a Saturday afternoon.

This led to a general discussion about attachment by children to their gender parent and what it might mean. I was privately remembering it was not so long ago that he had said he could remember nothing of any significance about his primary school days. Now he had suddenly remembered something of great significance through empathetic identification with his partner's young son. At the age of ten he had expressed the emotional journey of transferring his gender loyalty from his mother to his father – this is often seen as a necessary journey for boys, if they are going to become capable heterosexual men in adulthood. In the instance quoted above, there was the added complication that he was not the blood father of his partner's child. The boy's father lived in another town and saw his son regularly through a separation arrangement. However, my friend was the day-to-day senior male in the little boy's life, and was thus a significant male person in the boy's emotional life. The boy was clearly very attached to him, as he was to the boy.

I suppose the truth of the matter is that our memory function is very complicated indeed, and our capacity to remember every-thing consciously about our lives, as we grow older, becomes too much of a burden. So we need stimulus to call up significant memories and sometimes this stimulus acts spontaneously in the context of a particular moment of time, as it did in the above anecdote. Without the conversation and the presence of the man's parents, especially his mother, it is unlikely that the child-hood memory of 'hating' his mother would have surfaced. On the other hand, as a therapist I noted that he had initiated the conversation with his partner and mother present concerning the child's probable feelings in the near future and I wondered where that had come from. I did not feel it a sensible thing to enquire at that moment. Sometimes being a psychotherapist can be a social hazard and my reflections might well have stirred up other-wise hidden emotional material. The context, a friendly evening meal together, was not the right one. I fell to thinking about my own memory process and noted that as I grow older I remember the far past with relative ease, whereas I have to make out shop-ping lists when I go to get the groceries (something in the past I would have disdained to do!). As patients describe the past to me I remember concurrently scenes from the same period of my own life. For example, I have difficulty remembering what I did every day last week but I recall blissful holidays with my older brother (who has sadly died), on the sands at Dawlish Warren in South Devon, in 1938 and 1939, without difficulty. At that time it was a clean, unspoilt, natural landscape; idyllic. Of course these memories are now idealised. I shudder to think what it is like now. As I write this observation of disgust all sorts of other rich associations fill my mind, such is the power of memory and its associated mental activity! One year my wife and I took a holiday at my home town in Devon. I rented a relative's house and set about revisiting the past of sixty years ago. Much had changed but there was enough of the sameness to my memories to provide deep satisfaction. The surrounding countryside was still very beautiful, rich and verdant and full of wildlife. I came away satis-fied and happy, my mind full of the memories of a happy adven-turous childhood, spent in fields and lanes within walking distance of my home. So when we think about memory we have to relate it clearly to our stage of life development. I worked for a while with a very young, very distressed woman who had only fragmentary memories of her early childhood development. However, one particular scene with her father, when she was just entering her teenage years, is vivid and painful, moving her to tears of anger and distress.

The Client Remembers

In the psychotherapy and counselling room, although we give permission to our clients to remember without fear of our judgement, that doesn't mean that they will remember boldly and courageously or accurately the events and feelings from the past. As discussed above, a client might genuinely believe that she cannot remember childhood relationships with parents, siblings and friends, fearing unconsciously the outcome if certain emotions and actions are recalled and spoken of. And so there is resistance. Freud discovered a simple way of contacting the forgotten past. He asked patients to simply speak about anything that came to mind and, by association, work through ideas and memories as they arose.

This method came to be called 'free association'. Of course the therapist had a part to play in this process, and prompting and interpretations were used to assist the patient in the procedure. This has been a method not without its critics. The fear is that prompting and interpreting will lead the patient into the therapist's ground rather than into the patient's. This may happen and undoubtedly does from time to time. But my view is that the presence of the therapist is always influential and in circumstances where the client struggles, the relationship with the therapist is one of prime concern. We call it the 'transference relationship'. If the process of therapy is in the forefront of the therapist's mind she will be quickly alerted to the way in which a client may well abandon her own line of thought, in favour of a suggestion from the therapist. The truth is that the client's only real protection from manipulation lies in the integrity and capability of the therapist, and therapists are never perfect. It worries me sometimes how critical training therapists and supervisors can become when they find their trainee has made a 'mistake', either through therapeutic ignorance or just clumsiness. This can result in the trainee going into a defensive state, fearful of showing incompetence and of being wrong. It needs to be remembered that honest and open critical appraisal of our performance as therapists can only be accomplished in an atmosphere of trust, professional friendliness, and not blame. I think it is when our clients expose our own failures that we suffer the greatest discomfort and become most defensive Thus working with the task of recalling memories is a subtle and complicated process and the therapeutic relationship in the therapy room resonates with exchanges that are not always obvious in their meaning.

Example

Anna was silent in the session; she had been gazing out of the window, not looking through it, but rather looking at it. I wondered what took her attention so powerfully. I tried a short intervention but her gaze did not shift. I waited about another three minutes or so and she suddenly turned her attention to me. She repeated my intervention. 'No, you were way off the mark. I was watching the Battle of Waterloo!' I was surprised but I merely nodded and waited upon more explanation. I realised that my supposition that she had not looked through but at the window was possibly correct. She went on, 'There was a wonderful lithograph of the battle on the frontispiece of our textbook in the fifth form. Mind you, all a con. Wellington didn't win the battle on his prancing white horse, the Prussians did. They outflanked the French and that was that. The Brits took the credit, typical!' She snorted and grinned at me. I thought now where do we go from here? The material was rich with possibilities. Were we about to go back to her adolescence? The association of Wellington with her dad was another possibility.

A further complication that needs to be taken into account is the fact that the unconscious mind and the conscious mind are not discrete areas of activity. Indeed, influences from the unconscious play a strong part in influencing conscious thought and become features of experience in the conscious state without any recognition of origin. Similarly, conscious material can move into a state of unconsciousness almost before there has been a significant recognition of the material by the person concerned. Brown and Peddar in their authoritative publication *Introduction to Psychotherapy* (1979) discuss this phenomenon in some depth and much of what they said over twenty years ago remains true to this day. The interplay of mind experience between conscious and unconscious states needs to be reckoned with by the therapist, who, if sufficiently alert, will note the process in the client even though the client seems unaware of what is occurring. The traditional analytical method of 'working through' seeks to enable the therapist, in alliance with the client. The intention is to place analytical thinking in such a place of energy in the client's perceptions that the unconscious influence is exposed and becomes available to the client.

Example

A middle-aged male client spoke feelingly of a need he felt to achieve closer relationships with men friends. He was aware of a holding back. He was aware that he was only comfortable speaking to women of intimate feelings and experiences, drawn from the present and the past. In the middle of this speculation he suddenly spoke of his father with a degree of warmth and feeling that he had never displayed before with me. This was a very brief reference and quite suddenly he dashed off in another direction, speaking about work colleagues, his manager whom he admired and myself as his therapist. I let his monologue go on for some time and then rather cautiously I reminded him of the brief reference to his father in his earlier speculations. He seemed surprised at my remarks and admitted that he could not recall speaking of his father at all. I persisted in my suggestion and gradually he began to recover the abandoned ground of interest. He had 'genuinely forgotten' his earlier warm reference to his father. It had been repressed, although acted upon in the therapy room in reference to his managers and me.

This may not, at first sight, seem to be a significant anecdote. After all, it is the everyday stuff of communication in the therapy room, but I think his slipping in and out of conscious recognition of his father was significant and deserved the attention I gave it. The unconscious and conscious interplay was clearly evident to me but not to the person concerned. More importantly it gave my client an opportunity to think again about the reference to his father, whom he had forgotten, and to approach it with new emotional curiosity. It also helped me to remain interested in his son/father relationship. After all resistance can wear down the therapist and we can give ground that we should hold firmly. Or, and this is quite likely, we may have been taken obliquely into a discussion of his transference feelings towards me.

An interesting comment in an anonymous review (*Guardian*, 9 March 2002) of *Hidden Minds: A History of the Unconscious* (2002) by Frank Tallis, came to my attention as I was writing this chapter. In the last paragraph of the review, the reviewer states:

> In the end, he doesn't manage to show that the fact of unconscious processes in the brain equates to the existence of a monolithic Unconscious mind.

I am not sure that there are many psychoanalytic psychotherapists today who hold a view of a monolithic unconscious mind. My own is based on the notion of the mind being the dynamics of the brain in action. Therefore the conscious and unconscious would both be subjective experience of those dynamics, the word 'dynamics' implying a constant movement of thought and feeling promoted by the organism that is the brain. This in turn is influenced markedly by environmental events. It seems to me that the idea of distinct special areas of the brain being reserved for consciousness and other parts for the unconscious, in any *exclusive* way, is nonsense and does not equate with our subjective experience of ourselves as thinking and feeling entities. I also find the idea of a monolithic unconscious mind as a place rather like a vast psychic rubbish bin, full to the brim with relatively static memory material, mouldering away, both simplistic and disturbing. It is also vaguely amusing in a dark kind of way.

Dreams

Dreams (and dreaming) is perhaps our best access to the mind in its unconscious process. Freud (1957) believed that the dream offered a number of experiences. He thought that it protected sleep, except where we have a nightmare that wakes us.

Emotional energy that might well have woken the sleeper is expressed in dreams. The dream prompts memory. It has a presence in the form of images and sound that often works as a narrative, at one level, also being accessible for its latent content. This is unconscious feelings expressed in disguised or distorted form, available to the dreamer through psychoanalysis. The dream has no conventional framework of reference, and it has no respect for the conventions of time and space. In a sense, it has no past or present although it has frequently been associated with our memories of the past, sometimes even forecasting events to come. The thought of being admitted to the future might be an intriguing thought and, in a sense, such a projection might simply be a form of wishful thinking. Freud was undoubtedly right to emphasise the significance of dreams.

Example

Kevin had been sitting quite quietly and relaxed for a few minutes after entering the therapy room. I wondered if he had some special story to bring. He looked quite pleased with himself. He spoke: 'I had this dream last night, really interesting.' He launched into the narrative: 'I was out of doors on some kind of walking excursion, my partner was with me and quite a lot of other people who I did not know and now I cannot remember them clearly. Just a crowd. At the head of the walk was Alastair, my boss. Which is not like him at all. He is normally too laid back to obviously take charge of anything. Quite the contrary. He usually wants some stooge, like me, to act for him. And we, I mean I, do. But the funny thing in the dream was that I was quite worried because I felt he did not know which way he was going. We were lost but he wasn't saying anything. In the dream I did not mind being lost. I was more concerned for him, because I knew he would hate to admit to ever being wrong.'

Kevin grinned at me: 'Well, what do you make of that?'

As is my wont, I gave it back to him: 'Actually, it's more important for you to say what you make of it.'

Kevin smiled. 'Well, it's not him is it? I mean something else is going on. I felt really strongly I wanted to bring it here today, and that was unusual.'

I kept quiet and still, waiting.

Kevin went on: 'Like it was important for you to hear this dream and get the message.'

So I said: 'Well, Kevin, what is the message?'

Kevin: 'Well, put it like this, do you have any idea where we are going?'

I smiled. 'Got it in one!' More seriously: 'Does it matter if I don't?'

Kevin: 'I'm not sure. I want you to know. But how can you? I suppose it's for me to work out where I am going, if anywhere.'

He burst out laughing and there was quite a lengthy pause, a thoughtful silence between us.

And so we went on. Kevin, a pretty experienced client, knew that things are not always what they seem. He knew the dream had something to do with the direction of his life. He had strong ambivalent feelings about his boss, about me, and especially about his father, still a successful businessman, authoritative and managing in both his business and personal relationships. In the business world his father was a solid Labour Party supporter and an admirer of Tony Blair and the new direction of the party. Kevin, on the other hand, loathed New Labour and was not afraid to say so loudly from his unreconstructed socialist position. He and his father had had some tense and sometimes irritable discussions about contemporary politics, and Kevin recalled saying that Blair had no sense of history and no idea where he was going. When he connected this to the dream he chuckled and said: 'Well, that accounts for the fact that I was not worried in the dream.' Joining in, I remembered the anonymous crowd in the dream and murmured 'about focus groups'; we both laughed. Yes, I laughed too. I'm not afraid of showing some feeling from time to time, especially in reaction to a joke, even a feeble one.

This dream was laden with material at both a surface and latent level, and once Kevin felt free and easy with it he was able to freely associate towards it without any difficulty (Freud, 1957). And so the discussion went on drawing in his feelings about his father and me and his own sense of self and autonomy. It was interesting to see how a challenge to his deeply felt political beliefs resonated in his thoughts, producing strong feelings that needed expression.

As I write this I think of how rarely politics seems to enter the discussion in therapy or counselling (see Totton and House, 1997). The discussion of personal material appears to exclude political ideas as if taboo, whereas we all know that important political figures carry all sorts of projections of good or evil according to the view of the dreamer, client or therapist. Working for a while in Russia, towards the end of the Gorbachev period, I still met Russians who would excuse Stalin for all the crimes of the past on the grounds that these abuses would have never happened: 'If only Stalin had known what was going on in the labour camps.' This was a familiar remark, even made by innocent people imprisoned in the camps (Solzhenitsyn, 1973). Many were unable to believe that Stalin, this larger than life figure, an icon, the embodiment of kindly, eternal authority and communist humanism, would countenance such crimes against community, betraying his own people. His actions as a sadistic, murdering dictator were 'forgotten'. I often found him still portrayed as the father of the nation.

I think, too, that Mrs Thatcher played a part in the British collective unconscious, especially when she spoke of handbags and housekeeping – the concerns of a careful thrifty mother figure. Obviously she was not guilty of any crimes against humanity. However, the part she played in introducing radical right-wing monetary policies, which contributed towards massive change in our social structure with ensuing personal social misery for many, was often screened by a desire to see her as a sensible, well-balanced mother figure, who could manage the world about us, keeping us safe and secure. I leave readers to speculate what the youthful figure of Tony Blair might mean in a dream sequence that any of us might experience.

Freud was not at all reluctant to talk about the symbolic meaning of kings, queens, emperors, princes and princesses as they occurred in our dream life, and he often used them to indicate the nature of parental and child relationships. As I write this book I recall the weeks that brought many thousands of people out onto the London streets to witness the ceremonial around the death and internment of Queen Elizabeth, the Queen Mother. In a developing republican age many commentators have been astonished by the behaviour of so many members of the public in London. But a moment's reflection should reveal the obvious:

that the death of this royal figure stands for much that is of a metaphorical and symbolic character in the personal and collective psyche of British society. She was and remains an archetypal figure (Jung, 1978). For the individual the death of an 'old' mother is a significant psychological event. Life springs from the womb of the mother, she is the epitome of fertility and she can reproduce human beings, future kings and queens, and so her value is immense. Collectively, the death of a parent brings two important responses. Firstly, there is a kind of release from the past with this death. The surviving son or daughter is free: the future beckons with fresh energy. Then there is the feeling of immense loss. The world will be a different place, more hazardous then it was, and now we have to look to ourselves for survival. The death of this royal figure produced an intense societal psychical response. It appears that Mrs Thatcher could not have been more wrong when she asserted that 'There is no such thing as society.' It appears that we all share meta-memories, in this instance emerging after the death of the Queen Mother, that impel us to behave with deep feeling towards an event. A feeling that surprises us with its intensity and universality.

For Kevin, I figured powerfully as his therapist. I was his first confidant to whom, as he put it, he could 'say anything' but to whom he experienced mixed feelings of admiration, fondness and anger (especially when he felt stodgy, lost, not sure where he was going). I remained apparently unworried and, although friendly and caring, somewhat aloof. I was a significant figure in his process of remembering vital information, material lodged in his unconscious and pre-conscious, and if he was struggling and I seemed unavailable, he grew angry both with himself and me. I was working relationally with him. Although I worked in a friendly manner, I was not his friend and we both knew and acknowledged that as a fact.

I am conscious that in this section I have been leaning heavily on Freud and the culture of psychoanalytic techniques in making my points. However, I believe that the classical 'reflective' approach of the Rogerian counsellor, although easily parodied (as indeed is the silence of the analyst), will, if used properly, lead to material previously unremembered and thought forgotten. If clients are allowed and encouraged to explore their thoughts and feelings and memories, without intrusive therapeutic control, then the process of association will occur. Freud did not invent the process, he did demonstrate its usefulness. He did this when an assertive patient told him not to interrupt her flow of ideas and language (Freud, 1973). We should be grateful to her for having the courage to tell her doctor to 'Shut up and don't interrupt me!'

Very recently much the same scene occurred in my therapy room when a very disturbed young woman came for her sixth appointment and told me off. She accused me of 'leading her and not listening to her. She said the therapy work was superficial and I was too concerned with my own thoughts and didn't hear hers.' I swallowed hard and controlled a desire to defend myself. I decided to listen. To shut up. To listen as carefully as I could and think about what she was saying. After a further tense twenty minutes or so, some of it spent in total silence, I knew what I needed to do. I suggested that she should come and see me twice a week, rather than just once. I felt that her irritation with me was a reflection of the difficulty she was having in seeking under-standing of herself at a deep level, and that more time with her 'failing therapist' was required, not less. She was silent again for what seemed an age and then said: 'Starting next week?' I said, 'Yes, if that would suit you.' And that was that.

With approaching old age (as is the condition of this author), something interesting and rather worrying begins to happen. The memory for the immediate begins to falter. Ordinary common nouns become elusive. My wife and I play a game of 'wotsit' and 'thingimabob' to indicate we are struggling for quite ordinary words such as 'carrot' or tea. At about the same time memory for things long past seems to flourish, albeit in a very discriminatory way.

As a therapist I am astonished that in the context of the ther-apy room such blocks rarely seem to happen. I can still remem-ber the names of the clients, their relatives and friends and figures from their past without too much difficulty. So what is going on? I don't think anyone really seems to know. Quite clearly the cells in the brain deteriorate and fail and then there are consequences. But how does one account for the partiality of memory, that, for example, in one moment I can forget the name of an old friend, but in the next as I sit in the therapy room I remember without too much effort the biographical material of the client and her life? For years, outside the therapy room, I have had problems remembering people's names, and I have devised any number of games to prompt my memory. Mostly this forgetfulness was associated with mild anxiety in social settings. However, when I became a therapist the problem never seemed to occur in the therapy room.

Another feature of the problem of age is whether elderly clients are worth working with? Even if their mental faculties are not much impaired, have many of them the capacity for change, towards a healthier life, if they are inflicted with neurotic disorders of one kind or another? On an ethical level I find myself firmly advocating the right of elderly persons to engage in psychoanalytic psychotherapy as a means of dealing with distress. On the other hand I realise that in my small practice it is rare for me to encounter anyone over the age of sixty. Is that the watershed, unacknowledged by most individuals and the medical and therapy professionals? On a personal level I can report I re-entered therapy after the age of sixty and found it useful. Of course, some readers might be saying 'and what about the elderly therapist – which quite clearly this author is – is he too old to practise?'

I would again like to remind readers that clients have a right to silence and even to secrecy. I have mentioned earlier the perverse glee I shared with a trainee therapist as we shared a secret that we had no intention of revealing within the analytic group, of which we were members for three years. Any a therapist reading this confession would say, 'Well, they were just acting out.' My immediate cheeky response to that remark would be 'So what!' Obviously something was happening in the analytic group but what was the meaning of it? I think the meaning of it could only have been found in the moment of our transgression, safely explored within the group. But we didn't. About a year later we thought seriously about bringing our 'secret' back into the group, but somehow it seemed stale and irrelevant so we consigned it to a metaphorical waste bin. We couldn't even remember why we had been so amused at our 'acting out' in the first place. Perhaps we should stress that sometimes the internal supervision, as described by Casement (1985), is more useful to us then the open discussion we have with a colleague or supervisor. This is especially true when the moment needs understanding in the 'there and then', and we have to act upon our our emotional moment, whatever character it might hold.

Before concluding this chapter I wish to briefly discuss the question of the therapist remembering the client when the client is not present. Recently my practice has been disturbed by no less than three women clients suddenly becoming seriously ill, in each case with very serious possible consequences, including death. Luepnitz (2002) has described the situation in which a client experiencing, say, a panic attack can trigger empathetic responses in the therapist. It might be thought that the therapist has received and accommodated projections of intense anxiety from the client. However, what I have noticed in myself is that, although all three clients are temporarily (I hope) out of my care, being confined to hospital or home, I am carrying vivid anxious thoughts and feelings. Some of these are becoming internalised as memories associated with my own experience of hospital treatment some years ago as an adult and much further back as a child. I have remarked to my wife in the past how I appear to be able to 'forget' my more disturbed clients between sessions. But now I admit to myself that the presence of three of them, all experiencing dangerous and threatening physical disorders, stays with me as a palpable presence. I am unable to 'forget' them. I can, and do, resolve some of the tension by acting in a concerned way. In two of the cases the clients are therapists in supervision with me and I did not find it difficult to behave quite naturally and telephone them to express concern and seek some reassurance.

The third person was a client of some standing and at first I was not quite sure how to proceed. A friend of hers had rung me up to tell me that my client was in hospital following a minor stroke. I decided to confirm the situation for myself and after some initial difficulty traced my client through two hospitals and finally located her. I then wrote a cautious letter to her expressing concern and condolences and making it clear that I would continue to be available, if required, in a therapeutic way. Eventually we established telephone contact, and limited though that is, I felt it important not to let the physical trauma completely dislocate the therapy and my relationship with her. I found it reassuring and so did she. All this was achieved with some difficulty but I continued to monitor my own feelings and speculate concerning the level of feeling that had arisen within me when so much physical pathology had entered my therapeutic world with its regularity, predictability and security, which had all been cast to one side by 'events'.

Other pertinent memories came back to me. For example, my wife and I have had our fair share of worry when our children became ill, suffered accidents, cuts and bruises, and in one case a life-threatening encounter with a car. Both of us have at one time or another been to hospital as in-patients. It was almost as if my rather safe therapeutic family had been threatened with a major wound and I had a sense of immediate helplessness in the situation. It took a while to recover my balance and understand how to behave appropriately. And so memories of illness and hospital, which I thought forgotten, accidents and trauma spanning many periods of my life, were activated vividly by these unexpected events. I will explore this further in a later chapter.

Gradually common sense and insight did their work. I was restored to a more balanced position and was able to respond more rationally to the events that had occurred, that were just a matter of chance. The events carried no meaning of dark conspiracy, laden with death and destruction. I feel sure I shall gradually be relieved of these memories and they will be successfully 'forgotten' once again.

The emphasis upon remembering, which is a natural activity in therapy, can sometimes obscure our need as human beings to put anxious memories behind us, in order to direct our attention and energy towards our present and future destinies.

8 Projection: Touch, Transference and Counter-transference Revisited

How [do we] understand the link between public and private worlds, between our collective histories and the innermost, hidden, components of lives and minds.
Jacqueline Rose, Preface, *On Not Being Able to Sleep* (2004)

What belongs where and to whom? How do I know what I feel, and does it matter? How do I know that you really feel like that? These are some of the problems of personal and social identity.

Segal's book *An Introduction to the Work of Melanie Klein* (1964) gives a clear introduction to her theories and how she is attributed with the 'discovery' or 'invention' of the phenomenon of projective identification. Brown and Peddar (1979), however, point out how the awareness of projection was well understood by quite ordinary people many years before Klein made her 'discovery'. They offer the example of the anxious mother finding a great deal of her own insecurity and distress in the cries of her baby, and how she can't stand the strain of listening to what she imagines is the baby's appalling distress. However, in truth the child may simply need a change of nappy or a good feed. The mother in this instance may well miss the more obvious signals of hunger and discomfort. Or the mother may 'spoil' the child by responding to the child's every whim as compensation for her own poverty of emotional experience, dreading any evidence of the same occurring in her infant who she fears is at risk. Although my sources are over twenty years old the mental mechanism described is as common today as it was then. Most psychotherapists and counsellors come across this in their daily work with clients. Without wishing to unduly decry the work of Klein, believing that it is her followers who 'gild the lily' (for example,

Anderson, 1992), I am reminded of reading a letter written by Freud where he pointed out he was 'discovering' and describing emotional material that every common nursemaid already knew.

Example

I have written earlier of the person who came to see me, following a letter that her husband had written to me describing the urgency and pain of her condition. I eventually saw her at her own request. She wanted to see me because she believed me to be a 'kind' person. Her previous experience of therapists had been that for her they appeared detached, cold, emotionally aloof and basically not especially interested in her. She didn't know it, when she came, but she had stumbled upon a 'relational psychotherapist' who was challenging in himself the superficiality of therapeutic detachment. From the very beginning I was aware of the amazing contradictions of competing emotional states in my client. She would arrive, always on time, fling herself into an armchair and proceed to use her body to express the tumult in her mind. Her arms would flail about as she made word sounds, not coherent speech, to describe her internal world. She had walked to my house and yet asserted with vehemence that: 'I can't walk. Look at me, I can't walk. I'm in a terrible state. No strength. I can't do anything!'

The physical energy was manifest and I remembered Gloria Babiker's injunction to 'go back and remember the body' (Babiker, 2002). My client told me she knew why she was in such physical and emotional pain. She said her mother had treated her sadistically, beating her, screaming abuse every time she made a childish error. Her mother saw her as chaotic, useless and undermining of the mother's everyday life.

At this point I had no reason not to believe my client.

It was with some ironic surprise, therefore, that I learned my client had been a trained graduate scientist who had worked in an area where detailed precision was of paramount importance. So what was going on? She demonstrated internal conflict, and although highly intelligent, made entirely conflicting statements concerning her condition. I began to realise that her mother was actively alive in her personality structure, sometimes thrashing and hitting out guiltily in her super-ego, sometimes more rationally, complaining in her ego, and sometimes mumbling and howling within her unconscious desire for unconditional care and maternal. She remembered me as 'kind'. Inside her marriage all this came out in endless anger towards her husband, who could 'do no right for doing wrong' to coin a phrase. He retreated into distance, helplessness, social squalor and what amounted to an almost manic interest in an entirely compulsive hobby, the product of which came, gradually, to occupy a good deal of physical space in the house.

Example (continued)

My client was living out the consequences of frantic projections towards her on the part of her mother, which had continued throughout all her life, from earliest memory until she left home and went to university. She explained her marriage as coming about because she had thought her husband to be 'kind'. She also thought about me as being 'kind'. She admitted that on occasions, between her ferocious attacks upon her husband, like the attacks she had received from her mother, he could still be very kind, and she cited the occasion of his letter to me as an example, although she had virtually dictated it herself.

One of the major problems besetting the theory of introjective projection lies with the position of the therapist. I must admit that when working in a big NHS mental hospital, where many of the staff had only a rudimentary knowledge of psychoanalytical concepts, I used to get tired of hearing the clinical staff dismissing much of the interpersonal material they encountered when dealing with disturbed patients as coming to them as 'projection'. They believed the communication was fantasy based and not embedded in the real relationship with the therapist, whatever that might be. As a consequence the relationship with the patient was distorted, as the true weight of the so-called projected material was likely to be discounted. Although I understood this mechanism as a product of the imbalance of power relationships, which is so often encountered in a mental hospital, it did little to comfort or satisfy me in my relationship with my colleagues.

At another level I recognised that it is often difficult for any of us to sort out that which we are prepared to 'own' as properly belonging to us and that which is not. Sometimes it is confused because some of the communication we experience belongs in part to us as individuals, sometimes in part to the other. What muddle and confusion then reigns. It is sometimes inferred that the fully analysed therapist is able to clarify and make the necessary distinction of ownership. However, I am very sceptical about this. How many therapists are fully analysed, whatever that might mean? Often supervision will help but how many staff in busy NHS settings get the appropriate time and attention that such supervision requires (Feasey, 2002c)?

A point that arises from the above discussion is summed up in the simple question: 'How can I trust what I feel?' This implies that I cannot be sure at all times that what I feel is genuinely 'owned' by me. I think this often becomes most obvious during times of intense emotional activity, often in a social setting. I remember going to a wedding many years ago and for much of the time there I 'felt' uncomfortable, rather angry and dismayed at what appeared to be an uneasy alliance of a young man and woman. I also disliked the church service and the manner in which the priest enacted it (mainly, it seemed, for the benefit of the video cameras). Here I am, some forty years later, still remembering, with some shadow feeling lurking from the memory of that ceremony. As time has passed I have come to realise that my anger with the priest was misplaced. I was actually unreasonably angry with the young man. I liked and respected him. He had been one of my students in a college tutorial group. I had identified him as progressive, enlightened, well-informed and modern in his view of ceremony and morality. But here he was, kotowing, as I saw it, to the most banal of all expectations of the abused ceremony – that it should be organised as a good photo opportunity. He had let me down. What a criminal!

Another huge dilemma we face is how we can be certain at all times that we understand and properly recognise the feelings of others, especially our colleagues and, more importantly, our clients.

Example

John came to me with a number of complex problems. He is a mature artist, a capable one of some distinction. He makes a modest living from his work. Put briefly, it seemed he had a constellation of problems relating to a small number of women in his life. The most obvious cause of confusion and distress was the relationship with his lover, a married woman with two children. She claimed to love him but twice had tried to end the relationship. His mother was an object of affection and interest but she, too, had failed him, after the death of his father, by marrying another man whom he disliked intensely. The feelings were mutual. His mother had confessed to him her despair; the second marriage was a 'mistake'. The other key player in the family drama was a sister. This youngish woman, a talented academic, who worked mainly as a teacher, was very important to him. Unfortunately she was very neurotic and angry with her family of origin, who she thought to be dysfunctional. My confusion, as the therapist, came when my client John suffered a serious physical accident, which caused him to become an in-patient in a local hospital. He rang me to tell me and cancel his next appointment. He had also told his mother and his sister. To his amazement the sister had refused to come to the hospital to visit him, 'in case Mum is there at the same time; I cannot bear to be there with her'.

I felt a surge of hate for the woman coming from deep inside me, but the problem was yet to come. Come it did when I began to realise that John did not appear to hate his sister for her failure to come to his side, when he was clearly very seriously distressed. My basic assumption had been that he would have recognised the narcissistic character of her position in relation to him, and would have felt healthily angry. But it was not to be. My empathy was misplaced, and so I became angry with him for not feeling my feelings! It took me a while to identify his 'denial' and even now I cannot be sure of this interpretation. It seems too neat, too obviously psychoanalytical. A bit of hatred still lingers in me (see Prodgers, 1991). I realised that I had been drawn into the family dynamics and I needed to extricate myself if I was going to be of any use as a therapist to John.

Michael Argyle (1969) discusses the problem of personal and social identity for therapist and client alike. With this concern must come an awareness of the need for personal and professional boundaries, and how these may impede or advance a therapeutic position. I think this is especially difficult for therapists and counsellors who have powerful feelings of strength and certainty projected upon them and who may, if they do not approach this idealisation extremely critically, fall into the error of accepting these projections as being true and real.

Example

As I was writing this book I came into conversation with an experienced psychoanalytic psychotherapist whom, many years ago, I supervised for the last two years of his initial training. We were discussing a new entrant to the profession and I suggested some reservations about his intention of working as a psychotherapist, rather than to stay in his present, distinguished, academic position. My colleague on the phone listened to me carefully and asked me to amplify my remarks and so I did. I pointed out that on becoming a therapist and building a private practice I had gradually set aside, 'given up', a number of parts of my personal and social identity. I had always held radical social and political views and I had been politically active in my local community. I was known for this stance and both criticized and valued for the position that I occupied. However, I came to the conclusion as I moved into the culture of therapy that I could not continue in this committed public position as a community activist.

I am prompted to remember Philip Roth's powerful novel *The Human Stain* (2001), where the hero is a moderately successful academic who, like most of us, is concealing a place of shame in his life. He rides the situation easily enough with sufficient accommodations to support his position as a respected teacher in the local university. And then one day, quite innocently referring to one of his often absent students, he describes her in terms that unwittingly contain racist undertones (the word has changed from an old received meaning to a new, contemporary meaning, of which he is unaware). The outcome is that he is accused of racism and then faces a university disciplinary hearing. He could survive this if he were to apologise, acknowledge his latent racism and promise to mend his ways. But he won't. As a result he loses his academic title, job and status. He then has to fashion a 'new' life and proceeds to do so with all kinds of consequences. His personal identity (which is also social) and his professional identity (which, of course, is also private) are both seriously changed. He continues to nourish a powerful secret and thus the novel proceeds.

I quote this dramatic example simply because sometimes a life-determining decision brings with it a whole galaxy of unforeseen circumstances. These changes fashion the 'new' life in what can be a difficult shape and process. For my colleague, an artist and academic, I imagined his move from being in a public place of exhibitions that attracted attention, criticism and praise, to the somewhat severe denial of public acclaim of the world of psychoanalytical clinical work, would be difficult. I found this to be true for myself, but as the years have passed I have found some compensation, in part by writing books and articles and employing my radical views in examining the culture of psychotherapy. Of course, I am in a very different position to Roth's hero but, like him, I had to take a decision. I chose to give up my political activity and, eventually, a modest but engaging position as a freelance television presenter. I thought it inappropriate that clients could watch me on television on a leisured Sunday morning on BBC2! It is the act of taking a decision and sticking to it, with all its consequences, that is important and my artist colleague agreed it had been difficult for him, too. His social persona and private persona were changed by his decision to become a therapist, especially one working in the NHS. Although the pressure to conform is powerful within the culture of therapy, we were both left, fortunately, without a stain on our character, unlike Roth's hero.

The certainties that we sometimes enjoy when estimating our inner feelings and the feelings of others, believing them to be right, are sometimes quite unjustified. Carl Jung puts this well when he writes:

> We too can become dissociated and lose our identity. We can be possessed and altered by moods, or become unreasonable and unable to recall important facts about others and ourselves

so that people ask: 'What the devil has got into you?' We talk about 'being able to control ourselves', but self control is a rare and remarkable virtue . . . a friend can easily tell us things about ourselves of which we have no knowledge. (1978, p. 8)

Example

Alan, a man in his fifties, had been in therapy with me for some years. The bulk of the work was given towards his sexual identity and the quality of relationships he had with other gay and straight men, gay and straight women, and other colleagues. He had a lifelong relationship with his mother that was fraught and deeply engaging. His father was dead. Inevitably I figured as a father figure from time to time. He was also training as a therapist in a school of therapy, not my own, but sufficiently similar in ideology to avoid any clashes of style. He was a very successful professional man working freelance as a consultant in the public sector, concerned with children and families, and in this respect he made a healthy living. However, he was also keen to establish himself as a successful therapist. Towards this end he began to loosen his attachment to his consultancy and move with energy into the provision of therapy on a community level by establishing a centre for therapy in his neighborhood.

I had always seen Alan as a pretty robust figure and enjoyed my sessions with him when I felt he could cope with challenging interventions from me. This came about when I asked him to look more closely at his therapeutic ambitions and how they might be, in part, attached less to reality than fantasies of power and control. I was quite open about this and I knew I was taking a risk. However, I believed he could cope with this and benefit from it. So I was surprised when at the next session he came in angry and, I believe, hurt at my interpretation of his position as a therapist. He confessed that he had often been angry during this time of therapy with me, as I made comments and interpretations that seemed punishing or inappropriate. He also confessed to suppressing anger and to a desire to confront me with the concealed emotional material. I realized that sometimes my judgement of him and his state of feeling had been wrong. I realised, too, that my own feelings had sometime been misleading, and my judgement had been flawed.

At some level I wanted him to be a robust client who could spar with me, just as I had always encouraged other males to do, who were close and trusted companions. Thus the transference activity of Alan had been misunderstood and misinterpreted and blocked by my own counter-transference position for quite a long time.

In offering this example I am aware that the outcome of the exchange between us was finally therapeutic. He discovered his own desire to please me and a fear of revealing suppressed anger. I found my own emotional position of projecting onto him a fantasy that quite properly did not belong to him, but was derived from other truly more open and intimate relationships, some of which had been weakened by my profession as a psychotherapist. So in a sense I had been seeking gratificatory compensation in the therapeutic relationship. Now I am perhaps experiencing what Freud (1995) described as a 'condemning judgement'. I hope I continue to learn from it.

It would be wrong to leave the issues of projection and projective identification (Anderson, 1992) without giving some attention to the problem of gender. Freud suggested in some of his early writing that the girl child, realising she has no penis, is angry with her mother, to whom she attributes responsibility for this absence. The implication is, of course, that the child feels inadequate at the incompleteness of her body, as she witnesses it in her infancy. It would then follow that boys are envied for having what the little girl has not. Dinnerstein (1987), writing from a modern feminist perspective (which is usually very critical of Freudian theory), accepts that there is a 'core of truth' in Freud's observation. However, I have not come across much comment on the small boy's discovery that he has something that little girls do not – even though many, if not most, boys have participated in 'I'll show you if you'll show me' scenarios. I have found that the confusions and mysteries of infant sexual and gender development are sometimes most clear in the therapy room.

Example

A woman client reminiscing about her happy days as a ten-year-old child, playing with her best friend, recalled how both of them would ambush a fifteen-year-old boy and, running in front of him, would lift their tiny summer dresses and quickly lower their knickers, shouting out:

'Do you want a free show, Brian? DO YOU WANT A FREE SHOW?' Then, screaming with laughter, they would run away.

On the other hand she was quite terrified when her older sister's boyfriend, probably in his early twenties, wanted her to go to his place to see his puppy. She screamed and protested she did not want to go. But she did not reveal her actual fear that, if she did, he 'would do something to her', and that something would be sexual.

At this stage of her emotional, intellectual and social development she could hardly have been expected to differentiate between her pleasure at the sexual titillation of showing her vagina to a boy, and the secret anxiety of 'something being done to her' by a young man (a man identified as being a sexual creature in possession of her older sister). One can hardly describe her as neurotic but some of her behaviour, especially as expressed in the intense fear of the young man, might be seen as such had she been older.

She knew that her sister's boyfriend had got what she had not got, and that his penis was threatening. It could go into her. At some level she knew she had got what he had not got, a vagina, into which, to be satisfied, he must push his penis. After all, she had taunted the other boy with his need for the sort of 'free show' that only girls could grant – the power of the female!

What of the term 'empathy', the process by which we identify with another person? I have mentioned that my empathy was misplaced. It is a particularly difficult word because it is almost universally regarded as a benign process, whereas 'projection' is regarded as an unbenign, even pathological, process. And yet in both processes there is a high degree of 'the other'. In other words when we 'feel' for the other, believing our empathy is well placed, we cannot be absolutely sure that the state of feeling attributed to the 'other' is anything other than our own, originating in our own psychic history. This may not be too obvious to us, but as Jung says, it may be only too evident to others, friends, relatives, colleagues and the like. There is a common expression: 'I felt really touched by what she had to say', and this is often linked with the notion of empathy. In such a situation we might even reach out and touch the hand or arm or the shoulder of the woman concerned, as a gesture of recognition. In psycho-analytical psychotherapy this does not happen. Indeed, there is a very powerful taboo on the issue of physical contact between client and therapist. I have always found this of great interest. I am a trained psychodramatist, and in that therapy no such absolute taboo exists. Neither does it exist in dramatherapy where I have also been a practitioner. However, there is an absolute ban on touch in the practice of psychoanalysis and its sister creature, psychotherapy. Even the issue of the greeting handshake may be subject to close scrutiny in psychoanalytical supervision.

Why should this be so? Prodgers (1986) writes with feeling and insight on the subject. According to him, the traditional basis for the argument for not touching the client is that therapists are required to follow the dictum of Freud (who required therapists to work in the spirit of abstinence). It is argued that touch would undermine the purity of the transference, where the therapist ceases to be seen as a 'real' figure, but rather a figure of fantasy who carries all the infantile projections of the client. Therapy then proceeds by the analysis of these fantasies and their impact upon the interpersonal relationships of the client in her everyday life with those around her. This is a brief and rather crude account of the position of transference, but it is clear that the therapeutic culture has nourished the idea without appreciating that there may be a strong presence of unacknowledged fear of sexual arousal if touching takes place (see Prodgers, 1986).

There is currently discussion of sexual abuse between adults and children and adults and adults, and there exists a strong conscious level of anxiety among therapists that, in the privacy of their unchaperoned therapy room, they may find themselves accused if they stray from the most abstinent of positions with their clients. This fear may well be justified if the client is project-ing powerful feelings of a sexual character towards the therapist. To imagine the therapist won't respond is absurd. Readers will recall that I have described the transference/sexual relationship issue in Chapter 2 and here I am shifting the focus towards the problem of empathy and what I shall now call 'gesture'. Prodgers does not discuss in any detail the character of physical contact between therapist and client. The word 'touch' is used frequently in therapeutic discussion as if it only has one meaning, whereas we know that in practice we experience a wide range of physical gestures – some intimate, others formal (Fast, 1978). I can recall being somewhat shocked when I first noticed among Russian colleagues that even kissing on the lips between male colleagues was allowed. And there are a number of newsreels from Cold War days showing grim-faced Soviet leaders arriving at East European airports, greeting their counterparts, hugging them and kissing them warmly on the lips. On a personal level, in our culture, the most I would allow myself is a cool kiss on the cheek for some of my female friends/colleagues. Only a handful would get a brief kiss on the lips. As for males, well they would be lucky to get a pat on the shoulder, and perhaps on rare occasions a hug. With such a the level of inhibition in our contemporary culture, is it surprising that touching a client is taboo?

Gesture implies an action, probably of a relational character. We gesture to each other as a form of communication (see Argyle, 1969). The gesture can take many forms, from the total use of the body down to the smallest indication with a solitary finger. Sometimes, but not always, the gesture involves physical contact. When a client arrives at my house for an appointment I open the door and my first gesture is of welcome. I usually manage a weak smile. Then I stand well back to make it clear that the person is welcome to enter, at the same time moving away from the central position to give the required space for unimpeded movement by my client. As she walks pass, I usually make a physical gesture towards the therapy room with my right arm, inviting them to enter. It is my practice to allow the person a few moments alone in the room before I join them. If it is a first visit I enter the room behind them and indicate their choice of an armchair or chaise longue and I gesture with my hand where I shall sit. Then I leave them for a short time. I offer this somewhat obvious account of my physical activity simply to show that physical gesture carries a wide variety of shades of meaning. In this instance it is primarily intended to reassure and guide.

This is in high contrast to the anxiety (perhaps shame) that is evidenced by psychoanalytical therapists towards the gesture of touch which, irrespective of its context or organisation, is seen as an impediment to good therapy, being potentially (sexually) threatening (see Babiker, 2002, p. 12). I also have a disabled client whom I sometimes have to physically support as she negotiates the steps up to my house. It would obviously be callous, even sadistic, simply to watch her struggle on all fours to get into my premises. The boundary issue is addressed by this recognition of the potency of the gesture of touch and it seems appropriate to remind oneself that, in many respects, human skin can be seen as the final boundary between the psychic and material self.

The issue of 'touching' is seen very differently in the field of psychodrama. As a psychodramatist I was trained to touch the client, and it is commonplace in psychodrama to use touch as a means of identifying oneself and to reassure the protagonist (client) that she is not alone and has the support of the therapy team. Throughout a psychodrama there may arise a number of occasions where the therapist (director) touches the client using a range of physical gestures to support the drama therapy that is being enacted. The director is not the only person who touches. The auxilliary figures who play parts in the psychodrama (members of the therapy team or simply group members) are often called upon to dramatise through the dramatic gesture of touch. Interested readers will find more information and illustrative case material in my book on psychodrama (Feasey, 2001).

Most people will know the difference between being touched and being caressed. However, having said that, I am acutely aware of the subtle and not so subtle variations of touching. A close woman friend, in her seventies, went for a dermatologist consultation recently. She had a full body examination and the pleasant male doctor, chaperoned by a female nurse, when touching the back of her thigh said appreciatively 'Oh, what nice soft skin!' My friend was amused and pleased; she experienced a short frisson of sensual pleasantry at his remark and noted a little frown of disapproval in the nurse.

There is also a vast difference between the light touch and the firm touch, the hesitant touch and the confident touch (see Fast, 1978). We also discriminate between experience of the dry soft hand and the moist hand. There is, too, a wealth of difference between the intrusive hand and the hand that seeks permission before touching or entering our body. And then there is the issue of what part of the body can be touched. Most therapists will see their clients in the therapy room, with the clients either sitting on a chair or lying, fully dressed, on a couch. The greater party of the body is covered in clothes. But not always. Readers will no doubt recall my discomfort at a lecture when encountering Susie Orbach, the speaker, wearing a very small tight dress. In the proximity of the therapy room such an encounter may be even more powerfully felt (Orbach, 2003).

Example

Judith was a small energetic woman in her late thirties. She was married to a man older than herself, and had been for some years. For the greater part the marriage had been virtually sexless. She saw her husband as impotent in all senses of the word. He worked without enthusiasm in a factory, apparently devoid of ambition and appeared to share none of her interests, singularly lacking any for himself. Judith worked as a youth worker with very rough, sexually active working-class girls on a large council estate. She enjoyed the work, related closely with the girls, most of whom she admired for their flair, style, courage and 'guts'. She liked the way they handled their predatory boyfriends. Most of them were looking for a suitable 'fellah' to marry and have kids with.

The work in therapy wasn't all that difficult as regards her verbal dialogue but I found her non-verbal communication much more difficult to deal with. Judith was a bit plump and tactile. When she entered the house, although I was giving her plenty of space to pass me, she would inevitably come close, sometimes giving my arm a friendly pat. She would make herself comfortable in the armchair, in my absence, and when I came in I would notice it was a shade nearer to me than I expected it to be. As she sat cross-legged in the chair her skirt would ride up her right leg, exposing a generous length of thigh in sheer tights. She would wriggle and play with her skirt throughout the session. This made an uncomfortable impact on me and I struggled for the right words to interpret the situation to her in an unprovocative way; usually unsuccessfully.

The thing I was most concerned about was touching her without conscious intention, either as she came in or went out. I realised eventually I was actually afraid, in a shameful way, that

it might happen. I feared that it would be because my uncon-
scious, libidinously driven, would engineer contact as a response
to her pressure towards some physical demonstration of my 'love'
for her, in contrast to her libidinously deprived marriage.

Looking back now, I am amazed how tongue-tied I became, how stupid and incapable of finding the right words to say, to expose and render the situation safe and negotiable therapeutically. I am also taken back to Babiker's article (2002) and her concluding paragraphs where she spells out the therapist's dilemma:

We can feel enormous pressure from such patients to tolerate such an alteration in the boundaries [touching], perhaps by extending session time, or even by negotiating limited physical touch.

She goes on to say:

As therapists, we must be thoughtful about how our patients are involved with our bodies and minds. . . . This is a crucial framework within which to look at transference elaborations and transformations.   (Babiker, 2002)

I recognise that within the therapeutic experience with Judith I failed in this respect, although I do recognise that eventually she found a resolution that properly challenged her sexual life, riddled as it was with fantasy and voyerism. I shared with delight the erotic stories of her girl clients, although I realised that she was lacking any personal sexual life.

What strikes me now as I write this account is that Judith was 'showing' me her sexuality all the time she was in therapy and I was fearful of recognising it, hence my tongue-tied response. Babiker's plea for us 'to return to the body' may be interpreted in many ways and now I have moved far enough towards that position to allow myself to scrutinise my clients more confidently and thus speak that which was forbidden.

To conclude this chapter I would argue that as therapists we should not get too caught up with the problem of touch. I hope

it is clear that touch can take many forms. When we hug someone we are touching them; when we shake hands we are touching them; when we 'offer an arm' to assist someone we are
touching them; when we carry someone we are touching them;
when we pat someone we touch them; and a friendly punch on
the chest or shoulder is also a touch. These gestures are both real
and symbolic, and it seems that therapists are ready to negotiate
with the symbolic but nervous of responding to the real. Perhaps
they are still struggling with Freud's propositions concerning the
instinctive id-driven impulses we all experience (see Flanagan,
2003). And so it goes on. Physical gesture, too, may often be the
non-touching equivalent of the physical contact or a move
towards it. We are constantly 'showing' our relationships by the
use of our body. As a grandfather I am aware that the most
unafraid, non-sexually threatening physical contact that I have
recently experienced has been with young female and male
grandchildren. The enthusiastic lack of inhibition in such contact
is immensely rewarding to me. As I have grown older I have
allowed myself more physical freedom and I find the contemporary social gestures of public cheek kissing encouraging, although
we 'Brits' still tend to kiss the air, rather than the face.

I find it pertinent to close this chapter with a quotation from
Freud:

> In not a few cases, especially with women and where it is a
> question of elucidating erotic trains of thought, the patient's
> co-operation becomes a personal sacrifice, which must be
> compensated for by some substitute for love. The trouble
> taken by the physician [therapist] and his friendliness have to
> suffice for such a substitute.

Frankly I find no substitute in the sometimes opaque profes-
sionalism of some psychotherapists who seem to live in fear of
their own counter-transference. 'Intimacy between Strangers',
the sub-title of this book, is intended to focus upon the quality of
the 'love' of our clients and our felt response as therapists. These
feelings can exist without obscuring or confusing the therapeutic
relationship or putting either party at risk of betrayal. Freud's
choice of the word 'friendliness' needs to resonate. Not all intimacy is sexual although almost any intimacy can be sexualised. It

is incumbent on the therapist to work in a 'friendly' way in recognition of Freud's injunction, whilst at the same time resisting the impulse to sexualise. This is done either through self or provided supervision. It is done all the time between friends and relatives, and the degree of closeness and intimacy is moderated to that which is appropriate to the relationship. The words 'friendly' or 'friendliness' do not carry the same weight of feeling that the idea of being a friend does. Whilst the phrase 'I am not your friend, I am your therapist' is salutary, it still leaves room for the idea of being your 'friendly therapist', especially when it challenges the notion of being a sadistic or absent one.

9 The Unconscious: Dreams, the Imagination and Fantasy

We are such stuff as dreams are made of, and our little life is rounded with a sleep.

(*The Tempest*, IV.i.156)

Michael Jacobs quotes these words from Sigmund Freud in his recent study of him:

> the assumption that there are unconscious mental processes, the recognition of the theory of resistance and repression, the appreciation of the importance of sexuality and of the Oedipus complex – these constitute the principle subject matter of psychoanalysis and the foundations of its theory. No one who cannot accept them all should count himself a psychoanalyst. (Jacobs, 1992)

Of course, in writing this book I am taking a much broader view than Sigmund Freud did. There have, after all, been many changes in emphasis since Freud's day. A hundred years ago there was much emphasis on what he saw as the key features of analysis. Today, although these remain important aspects of the psychoanalytic view of the psychic development and life of human beings, new therapies and theories of mental structure and activity have evolved over the years, taking therapists off into different directions. What is surprising about Freud's stricture, however, is how elements of his theory still stand central to a wide range of psychological theories. With the exception of some of the more determined cognitive/behavioural theories, it seems that psychoanalysis in its many variations now colours the whole landscape of psychotherapy and counselling.

The notion of the unconscious and its place in the psychological life of human beings is still central to a wide range of theories. Even the most formal elements of clinical psychology teaching are somewhat reluctantly beginning to see the importance of the nature of the unconscious. As a supervising psychotherapist I have experienced all the common assumptions concerning the unconscious, as reported by a variety of psychotherapists and counsellors working from differing modalities (see Feasey, 2002c). I recently came across an article in *The Journal of Critical Psychology, Counselling and Psychotherapy* by Alison Tennant, called 'Where Angels Fear to Tread: An Experience of Therapy', and in her conclusion she reflects upon the presence of unconscious influences. This study derived from her work in therapy with a very difficult client, a case which found its way into the therapist's life as a 'punitive mother' in relationship to her own children. I was struck by this because I thought that, as a dialectical behavioural therapist, she might have given insufficient attention to the possible unconscious transmission of feelings, via projection, from herself to another – in this case her own children. It seems to me that the theory of an active unconscious mind, is gradually becoming more widely accepted among therapists. Now it is seen more a question of how much emphasis should be placed upon this phenomenon within the therapeutic dialogue.

Jung, who parted company with Freud over the centrality of sexuality within the framework of neurosis, did however stay close to the importance that Freud placed upon the presence of the unconscious. In writing about the subject in his *Man and His Symbols*, Jung puts the suggestion forward in a straightforward way: 'It is in fact normal and necessary for us to "forget" in this fashion, in order to make room in our conscious mind for new impressions and ideas' (Jung, 1978, p. 24). He then goes to make a more important and profound point:

> But just as conscious content can vanish into the unconscious, new contents, which have never yet been conscious, can arise from it. One may have an inkling, for instance, that 'something is in the air' or that one 'smells a rat'.

Although Jung progressed from these ideas and moved away from Freud, he still unreservedly endorsed the significance of the unconscious life. He tends, in my view, to neglect in the above remarks the thought that much painful material is 'forgotten', removed to the unconscious, simply because it is too distressing to remember it consciously. The anxiety of such material is too much for us to hold in our conscious day-to-day life, so we repress it, store it up at an unconscious level, where it may, to our eventual distress, remain active in more subtle and unrecognised ways.

Example

Geoffrey came to see me because he had occasional fainting fits. He had been through a range of neurological investigations but no pathology was found. On the advice of his supportive doctor he sought therapy as a means to explore his mind, both in its conscious and unconscious manifestation. Thus he looked for a psychoanalyst. No such person was available in our small city, but I was the closest alternative. Eventually he found me and we commenced work. He was rather surprised at first to discover I was not too interested in his symptoms. Rather, I wanted him simply to relax with me and to begin an inquisitive exploration of his life. Here he was a professional man, a successful senior partner in an accountancy firm. He was resistant to remembering and discussing his earlier life as a child. He was sceptical of its relevance to his present condition, a common enough assumption among many 'problem-solving' clients accustomed to working as managers in the here and now. After some weeks of relatively quiet remembering and reporting, he arrived at the next therapy session eager and somewhat distressed.

'It happened again, this morning, this morning, it happened. Again!' His voice rose infused with anxiety and excitement. He reported this to me as if he had found a lost jewel. 'Look at this,' he was saying; 'Listen to this,' he was demanding. He began to tell me the story. That morning he had his final appointment with the consultant neurologist who would be discharging him back to his own doctor's care. He had decided he would tell the neurologist about his therapy even though he was nervous that it would be received sceptically by the medical man. Nevertheless, he was going to tell him. His was the first appointment of the day

and he was sitting in the waiting room at 8:45 waiting to be called. At 9:00 he was called and, rather to his surprise, a pleasant young nurse told him to come with her. His consultant was not working in his usual room, which was being redecorated. And so they set off together and they walked and walked through a maze of corridors and he began to notice they were very close to some wards which he had never seen before. He told me it was at the point of seeing a notice that said 'Operating Suite' that a wave of nausea began to well up in him. He was embarrassed and said nothing to the nurse who looked at him and said cheerfully, 'Won't be long now, it's like a rabbit warren, terrible.' The nausea receded somewhat but he began to feel lightheaded. As they passed the entrance to another ward he spotted a chair and with a muttered excuse he walked over and sat down. He remembered nothing more until he came to on the floor, with the concerned nurse kneeling beside him.

I was quite amused at this telling of the event and I asked him to give thought to what had happened, to analyse it and see what the incident meant and how it had dramatised certain positions in his life. He quickly saw that the demonstration of the fainting fit at the very moment when he was going to be discharged, carried an important message for him and his medical consultant. He believed that now it would be difficult for the consultant to dismiss his need for therapy. Also he had an undisputed witness to his distress, in the form of the nurse. Now he would be taken seriously. After some discussion he also went on in therapy to remember an incident of frightening trauma, when he was an infant, involving hospitals and the forced separation from his hapless and helpless mother. Now he remembered the overwhelming terror that had overcome him when women and men in strange uniforms had came to prepare him for what his mother had described as 'the knife'! And so the therapy moved on.

In a sense, one can argue that like many other so-called discoveries in psychoanalysis the nature of the unconscious was known to everyone and yet, ironically, to no one. Freud brilliantly recognised it for what it was and suggested that it was an important guide to therapeutic procedure. And for this we should be grateful. However, I feel certain that a number of the counsellors I supervise, followers of Carl Rogers, will respond with as much recognition of the presence of the unconscious, as the committed members of the Institute of Psychoanalysis will. I must admit to being surprised when looking through the index of Irvine Yalom's early definitive work on group psychotherapy, *The Theory and Practice of Group Psychotherapy* (1975), to find no direct reference to the theory of the unconscious. This is surprising because even a casual glance at his reportage of case studies illustrates the presence of the unconscious in action within the therapy groups. In contrast, a recent book by Bill Barnes, Sheila Ernst and Keith Hyde (1999), described as an introduction to group work from the group analytic position of the English school, formerly lead by S. H. Foulkes, gives direct acknowledgement of the importance of unconscious processes, both at an individual and at a group level. The only real issue is how to use this knowledge. The psychoanalytic psychotherapist moves towards notions of resistance and denial (see Chapter 6). Counsellors and therapists from other models will encounter and recognise it, and respond according to the manner which they find most helpful to themselves and to their clients.

The unconscious manifests itself in other mental functions and it is especially present in the construction of dreams (Freud, 1975). In addition, we have wakeful dream states where fantasy plays a powerful part, and it is not surprising that normally unrecognised unconscious material plays a part in these. The most obvious aspect of this is what Freud describes as 'id' material. This material, sexual for the most part, strives for expression against much repression. This repression is based upon shame, fear and a deep desire on the part of most people to respect themselves and others as properly lovable human beings. One of the most obvious areas of such activity is the release of sexual tension through masturbation. Young men and women often find conflict between their desire to be 'good' loving persons and their need to explore the rich seams of their hidden sexual desires. Implied in that concept are all kinds of value judgements, mostly relating to moral and social attitudes, which are incorporated and expressed within our everyday culture.

Freud was not only a brilliant thinker, he was also a brave one. His instinctual theory, in which he identified powerful sexual drives of a primitive character, proved to be very difficult to advance, especially when he spoke of child sexuality. At the time it was probably this theory that cost him his much desired Professorship in Vienna. And of course being a Jew didn't help. Vienna was a hotbed of anti-semitism at this time. He daringly advanced what were seen as blasphemous and obscene ideas about the sexual world of children. We can note today the horror that is attached to any evidence of children being identified as figures of sexual interest either to themselves or others, and a great deal of adult and parental anxiety is displaced onto paedophiles, either real or suspected. As I write this, British Telecom is reporting thousands of Internet attempts to access child pornography, and our tabloid newspapers exploit these lurid stories to make ever greater profits. At the same time, a genuine academic interest in the developing sexuality of children is being repressed, passed over and, as a result, we have on ever-growing problem of premature sexual experience among children, leading to teenage pregnancy and sexual disease. Today, we are in the sad situation where many children, together with their parents, are ill-informed about their relationships with one another.

An interesting footnote to this story is the fact that when Jung defended Freud on the issue of repression and obsessional neuroses (see Jung, 1975, p. 172), he received a solemn warning from two distinguished German professors, telling him that if he continued to support Freud's theories he would ruin his career. Jung was very angry and retorted that if what Freud said was true, then 'I don't give a damn for a career'. Such was the tension surrounding Freud as he proceeded to elaborate his ideas in lectures, articles and books. Interested readers might wish to follow this discussion by reading Freud's letters to Wilhelm Fleiss (1995) where, with candour, Freud discusses his problems with a close and trusted friend.

Dreams

From these observations it seems sensible and inevitable that we now move on to discuss dreams. After all, it is in our dreams that we encounter much of the evidence for the unconscious, and especially for those elements that are repressed through our anxiety at entertaining them in the first place. Freud's writing is central to this discussion and indeed there is an argument that continues to this day concerning the significance of dreams and their relationship to the internal world we all own. I remember reading with some surprise a clinical psychology paper, about ten years ago (and long since lost) which argued that dreams are the equivalent of psychic rubbish that we trawl through and discard as we sleep. I thought such simplistic thinking about dreams was a thing of the past but apparently not. Set against this theory is the emphasis placed on the importance of dream life by thinkers and writers throughout the ages. The 'interpreter of dreams' has always been (and remains so to this day) a significant role in our communities. Emperors and beggars have sought understanding and knowledge through recounting dreams. We often encounter in our popular press reports of people who claim to have avoided a calamity – such as a rail or air accident – through heeding a warning given in their dreams. We may all be sceptical of these claims, but the presence of the dream as an experience of significance and value is hard to deny.

Example

A youngish professional man came to me much distressed. He said he had a sexual problem. He was in a long-standing relationship with a young woman, about five years younger than himself, but their sexual life had dwindled to virtually nothing and plans to marry had now been seriously questioned, especially by her. Hardly surprising. One of his greatest problems was that, although he felt no sexual drive towards her, even though he claimed she was a very attractive woman and other men envied him, he had sexual dreams which invariably ending in orgasm in which she presented as a figure of great desire. He found this paradox very disturbing. On occasions this dream, or a variant of it, happened when she spent the night with him in his bed and when he had felt no conscious desire towards her. There were other deep problems in the relationship, not least her over-involvement with her mother and father, especially the latter. For a number of reasons I decided not to take the case but to refer him onto a couples therapist, who I knew would work with the dream material, seeing it as valuable therapeutic material. The girlfriend was eager to do this and so they went off to the other therapist. I had every confidence in the therapist concerned, a very experienced woman, but my main point of confidence was knowing of her interest in dreams and the place of the unconscious in our lives.

Freud described the dream as 'the royal road to the unconscious' and for him the task of understanding dream material was seen as essential to any analysis. I am not so sure if this is still the case today. Working as a supervisor I find I am often prompting supervisees to take notice of the dreams of their clients. I noticed when working with a community in the NHS that not much was said about dreams by patients or therapists. In my reading across a wide spectrum of therapies it seems that these days dreams are rarely presented as significant material. In one contemporary book on group analysis I saw only a few sentences on the subject of dreams, and I have noticed a rather disturbing absence of interest in dreams and their meaning in general in the literature of psychodrama and, to some extent, also in dramatherapy and other creative therapies.

It may well be that some of the current techniques for working in therapy do not encourage the exploration of fantasy in a free associative manner, which Freud felt was the way in which dreams should be approached. I think it is highly unlikely that cognitive therapists, centred upon behaviour and behavioural adaptation, would find their way to dreams very easily. Even if they did, how would they work with what is presented? I do not think sex therapy based on the work of Masters and Johnson (1985) would have helped the client referred to above. What is sometimes described as ego psychology seems now to dominate some areas of psychotherapy work where the conscious meaning is all important, and clients are helped to understand their dysfunctional emotional behaviour in a social context, and to look for adjustments to that behaviour to improve personal and social relationships. Of course, this is a good thing, but I believe that sometimes it leads to frustration and inadequate outcomes and a failure to satisfy the client, who may feel that something has been missed. Indeed, something may well have been missed, and this may well remain in the client's subconscious, ready to surface again in various guises. As for counsellors, this non-directive approach to their clients can provide a good opening for the discussion of dream material. However, then it is a question of how the counsellor feels and works in respect of presented dream work will that determine the possible outcome of the therapeutic exchange.

The dream, with all its various levels of activity and representation, is valuable because it represents an on-going process of psychic activity that has significance to the dreamer, even though this is not immediately recognised by her. It contains messages that are both welcome and unwelcome. Judgement doesn't really matter to the dreaming unconscious mind, as it strives against distortion and repression to have its say. The young man described above could not avoid the strange message that seemed to be saying 'yes, you do have strong sexual desire for your partner, but something in the relationship threatens you and cuts you off from those intimate feelings, and prevents you being close in a sexual/intimate way.' Even in the short interview time with me it was obvious that closeness and dependency were difficult issues for him, especially those within his own family.

Dreams sometimes have a straightforward narrative content unambiguously clear to the dreamer, who is able to understand their significance immediately upon waking. On the other hand, a dream may work only in terms of metaphor and symbol, and here the dreamer, once awake, must find the key to understanding its meaning (see Jung, 1975). Freud believed that 'free association' of the ideas and images in the dream could lead to greater understanding. It is my experience that clients vary widely in their ability to work in such a way, and I think a certain kind of self-confidence is required to explore the image, vision, sound or smell, and reach an acceptable conclusion. This is where the work of the therapist comes into play in a very powerful way.

Example

Jim, a man in his fifties, was disabled after a motorbike accident and his severely damaged leg, twisted and distorted by multiple compound fractures, made walking a trial and prevented any sporting activity. The latter was a great loss to him, as he was an enthusiastic amateur football player, who usually played in the forward position as a striker. He worked with me for some years and on some days he would cheerfully settle himself in the therapy room chair and grinning at me say: 'I've had it again.' What he meant was that he had dreamed the night before of playing and running and scoring goals with a perfectly functioning pair of legs. Simple-wish fulfilment it might be said. And that would not be wrong. But there was always something else. Usually it occurred in the detail of the dream and its context or feeling. It was the manner in which Jim dealt with the dream that proved to be so useful in his therapy work. He would quickly notice the apparently insignificant or obscure, addressing it with interest, which usually led to a clearer understanding. In this instance it was related to sexual frustration, issues of masculine power and his difficulty in attracting and managing relationships with young women.

The interpretation of dreams is immensely rewarding but it requires patience on the part of both client and therapist. Sometimes I have been asked: 'If Freud insisted that dreams represent desires, how did I come to have this intensely worrying dream, a dream that comes regularly in which I always suffer anxiety? How can this be wish-fulfilment?'

'How indeed? The answer is always particular to the client. It is a truism that what is sometimes deeply desired is also sometimes equally deeply feared. A client, an ex-soldier and survivor of the Second World War (where he had experienced the horror of warfare in which he had been actively engaged) had terrifying dreams. The dreams were almost nightmare in presentation. He would wake from them sweating. One day after reporting such a dream he suddenly said: 'Of course, I notice in the dream I am always the survivor.' This from a man who had seen all his friends die or suffer terrible wounds. He had survived.

The presentation of unacceptable material is common in dreams. Nowhere can this be truer than in the instance of sexual desire, which does not respect such civil niceties as marital love, faithfulness and monogamy, or the age or sex of the desired figure appearing in the dream. It is common for a devoted husband, wife or partner to use the dream form to express 'hate' for the other partner. Such hate is unwanted in the conscious mind where it is met by fear, guilt and denial. It becomes unsupportable and is repressed only to return disguised in the form of a dream. We know that dreams conflate psychic material, sometimes distort it, even censor it, when the dream experience threatens to become a nightmare, a state of sleep psychosis from which, thankfully, the dreamer awakes. So the notion of wish-fulfilment goes beyond the simple expression of pleasure towards states of mind that the dreamer, awake, might be reluctant to acknowledge and own.

Sometimes there are dreams that appear to defy analysis. Often dreams that are almost entirely symbolic, full of shape and colour but lacking any social references, appear so abstract that they apparently stand alone, almost unconnected to the dreamer. But this is where the technique of free association finds a valued place. One is asked to respond spontaneously, almost as if standing in an art gallery in front of a pure abstract painting. The viewer has to rely upon personal response to engage not only with the image but the self as the viewer. The therapist stands in such a place with the client, listening carefully and sensitively to the client's remarks, only tentatively interpreting when it is clear that the client would welcome a therapeutic reflection. It is at this point that the terms 'perhaps' and 'maybe' come in useful.

Imagination and Fantasy

In the title of this chapter I speak of 'imagination' and 'fantasy'. How do we distinguish between these two states? At this point I turn to the *Pocket Oxford Dictionary* for some help. It describes 'imagination' as:

1. mental faculty of forming images or concepts of objects or situations not existent or not directly experienced;
2. mental activity or resourcefulness.

It describes 'fantasy' as:

1. imagination, especially when unrelated to reality;
2. mental image, daydream;
3. fantastic invention or composition.

As you can see, dictionary definitions are of limited use in the context of psychotherapy. For example, the word 'imagination' is often surrounded by a hue of approval: we often praise works of the imagination as they occur in the visual arts and in literature, prose and poetry. Dance, too, is an area where the concept of imagination is valued. Creative imaginative drama, especially with children, is regarded as a valuable, cherished educational experience for children and young people. Rewards such as personal growth in self and social confidence are often seen as possible outcomes. And so on. Fantasy, on the other hand, usually has a more mixed reception. Although it can share with the word 'imagination' some of the same preferred qualities, it can also be associated with pathology. For example, a murderer suffering a paranoid delusion may be said to act out a murderous fantasy arising from paranoid anxiety. However, in no circumstance would you find the term 'imagination' used in that context. In psychotherapy theory the word 'imagination' is rarely used other than as a personal quality, perhaps relating to some artistic or cultural aspect of a client's life. Here I shall observe these distinctions but not in any absolute sense of fixed meaning, if for no other reason than the fact that the character of English language allows and encourages all sorts of shift of meaning according to contextual use. The other major distinction I shall make is that 'imagination' is closely associated with creative activity and production; 'fantasy' is less so. Indeed, a lot of fantasy lies undetected within the individual – it occupies a private place within the psyche – whereas imagination often demands expression, even in the earliest stages of development of human beings.

Example

I was travelling on a crowded commuter train from Leeds to Manchester. Across the gangway was a large woman, heavily burdened with packages, accompanied by a lively three-year-old boy. He sat still, being 'good' for the first twenty minutes of the journey. Then he became restless and wriggled on and off his seat, disturbing his rather weary mother each time he did so. She remonstrated with him each time and for a while he respected her admonitions to sit up and sit still. Eventually he got off the seat and stood in the narrow gangway between the rows of seating. He was now close to me. I could watch him quite unobtrusively. He seemed to go into a shallow trance and his little arms and hands began to touch the back of the seat in front of him, following a pattern. At the same time he began to pull faces and make noises. When the train reached its first stop at Huddersfield it began to slow down; the braking effect could be felt and the sound level changed. In response, the small boy began to mime energetically pulling levers, twisting handles; his noises became more apparent. Of course! He had been driving the train and now he was bringing it to a halt. All had been imagination but it had been worked out as benign action through a small mime drama. It had served a purpose in occupying his attention, engaging his frustrated energy and his internal world of imagining. It had also kept him out of trouble! Little boys still want to be engine drivers.

I believe we, too, as adults hold on to imagined scenes of activity. Sometimes we do it to prepare ourselves for action. A good example of this is when a person is summoned for an interview for a highly desired job. The person concerned begins to rehearse a presentation of the self and the likely character of the interview. All this takes place internally, unobserved by outsiders. Finally, the moment of the interview comes and the imagined rehearsed material comes into play dynamically, with much modification of psychic energy. The psychotherapy of psychodrama (see Feasey, 2001) makes good use of this phenomenon and it is commonplace for the participants to imagine and rehearse either old or new situations for the commentary of the psychodrama therapy group. Closer still to the therapeutic world is the place of art therapy. Working in a therapeutic community alongside an art therapist I was always struck by the depth, sophistication and worth of visual art activities carried out by some of the patients. Many of them were from deprived socio-economic backgrounds and would have had little experience in handling such art materials (and this in itself can represent a challenge to the naïve and inexperienced user). However, the pursuit of therapy seemed to liberate the patients, and they often produced highly imaginative artwork. One of the most striking things was the remarkable use patients made of the insights they had gained (or were on the process of gaining).

Example

Joan, a private client in her third session at the hospital therapy centre, said she would like to bring some artwork she had produced some years earlier with a therapist who often worked with art products. I knew and valued this art therapist and so readily agreed.

Encouraged by her previous experience of psychotherapy, Joan had come to me wanting to take stock of her life, both personal and professional. She was an actress and quite a successful one, working with a distinguished company. But she claimed to feel deeply dissatisfied with her world of theatre, with its performers, directors and management. She also had quite complicated family problems. She was single, attractive and energetic, with a good group of friends and a lover. He was married and very firmly attached to his family, which consisted of a wife and three children. Joan claimed not to want to act destructively destroying his status quo. She also spoke of the satisfactions of her acting career where she appeared to be doing well. I was rather puzzled by her presentation. Her intelligence and insight were apparent. Her family problems were no worse than those suffered by many others. Her support system seemed pretty good and she claimed to be satisfied sexually. But her emotional life seemed insubstantial although she said she loved her lover. On the other hand she did not appear to want to bring about radical change in that direction.

Then the day came when she brought in her paintings. All were abstract, strongly coloured and geometrical. The firm boundaries and tight clean representation of the watercolours struck me. We talked at random. I allowed her to lead the way and went most of the way with her conclusions and reflections. It was only many weeks later, after the artwork had been put aside, that I began to reflect again on the paintings and felt the separateness of the colours and shapes in the paintings. The boundaries seemed impermeable, lacking all flexibility. I remembered, too, how the paint occupied all the space in the picture. There were no borders of plain paper, no overspill, no way out. I knew it was important to return to these images for more consideration.

I have been intrigued by Jung's account of his imaginative and fantasy conflicts as described in his *Memories, Dreams and*

Reflections (1975). Here he described the conflict between his romantic imagining of the presence of God as a king on a throne in heaven surrounded by equally striking and attractive figures, and the fear that the sight of the black robed monk could evoke in him (1975, p. 29). Attached to the monk image were fantasies of hatred and punishment, which in associated with his father. This description seems to support my general view that the meanings we attach to the words 'fantasy' and 'imagination' can have very different emphasis, sometimes of an emotional and moral character. Psychoanalytic literature is full of such reference. For example, Michael Jacobs's reader, *Sigmund Freud* (1992), gives generous attention to 'fantasy' in the index. Klein's *The Psychoanalysis of Children* (1932), in particular, places enormous emphasis upon 'fantasy', especially in its passive form, as a set of internal mental mechanisms. As regards 'imagination' Freud attributed little importance or psychic value to its productive activity (see Mitchell, 1995, p. 25). Given his well-known interest in art, especially small sculptural objects, this is somewhat surprising.

It appears that the activity of fantasy, whilst colouring attitudes and feelings (especially in interpersonal relationships), does not often lead to a discernible product whereas the use of the imagination does. In dramatherapy (Jennings, 1973) a relaxation exercise may be focused upon a passive trance-like recollection of a beautiful or happy scene where the subject has known peace and happiness. On the other hand, in dramatherapy the imagination often springs into life as a series of observable tangible acts and representations. Here, there is no clear boundary between the imagined and action. It is the observation of such action in the context of the imagined situation that provides valuable therapeutic information for client and therapist alike. Perhaps our academic psychologists will eventually take note.

10 Reflection

When we reflect upon the past we are putting things together, making connections from the past to the present, of thought and feeling. We look for an understanding of actions in retrospect, invoking our beliefs, thoughts and feelings in order to connect with the conduct of our lives.

I am indebted to Emmy van Deurzen-Smith (1984) for the following reflections on the person of the therapist, which appeared in *Individual Therapy in Britain*, edited by Dryden (1984):

> The therapist's personal life is of great importance, as a journey towards becoming truthful and authentic has led the trainee through various crises that have been dealt with inventively and creatively. Times of despair, anxiety and loneliness must be a living reality that she can struggle through successfully.

Here, Emmy van Deurzen-Smith is writing about existential therapy and attributes these qualities as necessary to the existential therapist. However, to my mind they are applicable to all psychotherapists who have been trained through the process of personal therapy and counselling. The whole ideology of existential therapy is imbued with a preoccupation with philosophy, as well as psychodynamic psychology, and it seems to me that all psychotherapists are concerned with the different levels of what we call 'understanding' as we pursue our life paths.

Many years ago I studied for an MA in Modern English, where issues of a philosophical character were actively pursued, and one of the most important aspects of the course was an indepth examination of existentialism within the context of literature. Now, 30 years later, I find that learning experience just as influential to me as it was then. What is so striking about the quotation above is its emphasis upon the journey and the vicissitudes that all human beings experience, in varying character and degrees, as they make that journey through life towards the inevitability of death. As a consequence, I suggest that van Deurzen-Smith's remarks are applicable throughout the whole world of psychotherapy practice, from whatever discipline and model it proceeds, whenever a psychodynamic process is active. Such a realisation and acceptance must have a profound effect on the practice of psychotherapy, where the therapist is inevitably drawn into the drama that is every person's life.

Freud and Friendship

In Chapter 6 I quoted Freud on the nature of the relationship between therapist and client, especially where he used the concept of 'friendship'. One of the characteristics of friendship is the empathetic sharing of experience. We might find ourselves nodding in agreement when a friend describes an experience from their childhood. These nods suggest that we are sharing the experience and consequently acknowledge its validity in the life of the friend. Our experiences do not need to be exactly the same. However, what is needed is a confluence of experience that confirms the importance of felt experience, recalled at a later time of life. The implications for the contemporary psychotherapist are obvious. Whenever a client is describing to me the conditions of her life as remembered from infancy I find myself in a parallel world of personal experience that mirrors (or contrasts) what I am hearing from my client. This produces feelings, and these enter into my relationship with the client. Similarly, events in the clients' lives, contemporaneous with therapy, will resonate with my life experience, either of the present or the past. This is especially true for me as I am much older than most of those who come to see me. Sometimes this is technically called 'counter-transference', but as a word I find it much too limited to account for the experience of the therapeutic relationship with my clients. In some respects, the feelings I have are not the result of transference at all: they are more a reflection upon a common experience.

Example (see also p. 132)

For some unknown reason my private practice was at one point invaded by critical physical illness. The presence of life-threatening disorders in three clients cannot be accounted for other than by unhappy coincidence. In each individual case it may have been possible to find more satisfactory explanations for these illnesses, and no doubt the doctors caring for these clients did their best to look for causes as well as effective treatments.

However, the coincidence of these three clients with their serious illnesses caused me unease. There were professional problems. One client was so ill that she withdrew completely from working professionally with me. Her withdrawal was very quick and came without warning. How should I react? What should I do? Should I cut off communication? Should I maintain contact in a regular, but unobtrusive manner, by telephone, making no charge for my attention? It was very likely at the time that she would recover from her illness and I thought she would return to me but it was my feelings at that time that I had to struggle with.

Another client had a sudden illness. He was taken as an emergency to a local hospital some miles away and after a short time of diagnostic examination he was moved to another hospital, again some miles away, where specialist treatment was available. I was informed of these events by a friend of my client who, on his behalf, revealed some personal material about my client that affected my feelings about the events very strongly. What should I do? Should I pursue his progress from one hospital to another, with polite restrained enquiry, not revealing who I was to the medical staff? Should I attempt to speak to him by telephone?

The third of these clients suffered a completely unexpected physical crisis, which led to unpleasant and unsightly surgery. In this case she was able to come and see me and tell me about the situation and we were able to face the trial that awaited her together. She was able to come for a number of other sessions, while awaiting surgery, and I found that I had very different feelings about her and her situation.

The truth is that I felt very disturbed by these events. Through the progress of the psychotherapeutic relationships with these clients, I had received many projections that resonated with and activated my own memories of parallel anxiety (Humphreys, 2003). Having experienced the deaths of several elderly relatives over the last few years, I have become accustomed to the presence of death on the doorstep. However, I know as I write, this bare statement that fails to convey the sense of loss and sadness that inhabits me as a result of these losses. So when my practice was suddenly engulfed, as it seemed, with more potential loss I found my self confused and worried, struggling to know how best to respond. Where did the personal and the professional begin and end? To use the word 'reflection' again, in a rather different way, I have reflected upon the circumstances and my response to them.

The events are not in themselves transferential. They spring from realities beyond the power of my clients, unlooked for and unwelcome. These events are not attributed to me or my work as a therapist. However, they do impinge forcibly upon the nature of my relationship with these clients who, I feel, see me as a person with a responsibility to care for them. So our feelings for our clients can take us well beyond the phenomenon of transference. Some of these feelings may need the attention of a professional fellow therapist to work with, or expert supervision. Certainly, the immediate issues of professional response will need intelligent sensitive supervision. This may either take the form of self-supervision, as discussed by Patrick Casement (1985), or external supervision with a competent supervisor (see Feasey, 2002c). On the other hand I suppose we may have to accept the remarks of Emmy van Deurzen-Smith (1984) quoted above, and simply accept that as therapists we need our fair share of existential pain, and that we need to manage it as best as we can by drawing on our own personal resources.

The other feature mentioned earlier is that of parallel experience. Although there may be some concrete experiences that we share, without comment, with our clients (a day-trip to the seaside as a child) there for example, other parallel experiences that are more deeply felt, and which hold a great deal that is personal and subjective, not necessarily shared with our client at all. This experience needs careful handling. Often this material comes from our past and it is a particular moment in the therapy room that recalls it into memory, as a thought and an emotion that needs to be recognised. The past and the present are for the moment brought together, connected and present as a conflation of thought, memory and feeling. Virtually all therapists and counsellors will experience this situation at some time, and most of us have the ability of holding it in ourselves (albeit sometimes with difficulty). But my point is that it adds to the pattern of our interpersonal relationship with our client. It may never be openly acknowledged but it will make its presence felt both consciously and unconsciously.

Petruska Clarkson (2000) writes of this experience when considering what she describes as 'Complementary proactive counter-transference', whereby the therapist finds herself replicating her own past in the relationship with the client. Although I, too, have suffered critical illness in the past, the problem for me when dealing with the critical illness in my clients is that the feelings that arose for them were of here and now anxiety, brought about by a frightening event. Although for the suffering client memories may be evoked that are painful and confusing, there is present a stroke of fate, not from the past, but a product of an ominous present. Thus, it is not archaic material being projected towards me from their childhood experiences – rather it is a realistic threat that needs management in the therapeutic relationship. At this point I think of Freud and his suggestion of the comfort of friendship. I am quite sure that a cool absence of myself in the relationship is not called for.

There is a vast body of writing on transference and Clarkson (2000) is an authority on the subject. However, very little is said about the fact that, as therapists, we daily encounter material that is not projected onto us from historic relationship that our clients experienced in their childhood. On the contrary, as Harold Macmillan once said ruefully, referring to disturbing experiences from a time when he was prime minister, 'It's events, dear boy, events!' Our own lives as therapists are full of events in the same as clients' are. This presents in our therapy rooms as material that needs dealing with, in one way or another. Often the literature of counter-transference is not immediately helpful in this respect. Frankly, I find it distressing that some psychotherapists seem to actually distance themselves from their clients who are suffering critical illness, which confuses and stresses the therapeutic relationship. I feel quite sure that most contemporary leading therapists and counsellors would abhor such an unfeeling response.

Recently a supervisee of some standing, a counsellor, surprised me somewhat by asking me how he could direct a client to her past. The client in question was about 26 years old, but appeared much younger, quite child-like and small and frail. She spoke fleetingly of sexual abuse but was inconsistent both in her attendance at counselling and in dealing with issues in her life. We discussed ways of improving her attendance by drawing her more deeply into a trusting relationship with him. My supervisee still seemed rather worried about the issue of how to get her to address her past. Our session was nearly over and I tried to give some final practical help: I said, 'Well, ask her is she can make any connection between what is going on in her life now, with any event from the past.' He seemed relieved to hear me say something so simple and directive. I hoped it would work but at the same time wondered what was happening to him, in his relationship with her, that had led to this sense of helplessness in him as she strove to avoid past trauma and the dynamics of family distress. As the session finished I heard him remark, more to himself than me, 'Oh my god, families!' Indeed.

Making connections is one of the prime tasks of psychotherapy. It is also a major matter of concern for all human beings in whatever level of life they find themselves. Sometimes we find ourselves remembering the pain of the past, more often than not experienced in failed relationships, and we vow to avoid repetition. However, disappointment comes when we once again find these repetitions once in our lives. We curse our fate whilst at the same time guiltily acknowledging our personal inability to 'learn from the past' – which is something we are so often invoked to do by well-meaning friends and relatives. In therapy the client is free from such admonitions. Here, instead, the therapeutic task is to unfold such repetitions by subjecting them to rational and emotional scrutiny, free of blame and guilt. As free as we can hope to achieve in such a setting.

Example

Jane had been brought up by a nagging, obsessive, housewife-cum-mother. Her childhood was barren of outward demonstrations of affection from her mother, although at some level she thought of her mother as loving her, and the admonitions were, as her mother put it, for 'her own good'. The home was cared for with fussy attention to ritual and detail, to the extent that her father and herself found themselves cowed and slavishly obedient to her mother's cares and whims. She remembered being rather secretly scornful of her father for silently putting up with the day-to-day nagging. She also believed, as adolescence approached, that her parents had only had sex once, of which she was the outcome. She thought her mother would think of it as being a very messy activity. These were all secret thoughts tinged with anxiety and guilt. She never confessed any of her feelings to a best friend at school. She suffered her mother's neurotic control and, in order to avoid trouble, decided not to protest too much. She felt she could not rely on her father to back her up. She thought, probably rightly, that he would support his wife to avoid bigger problems for himself.

Jane was very open with this story when she first arrived for therapy and often reported these memories to me when they seemed to fit other issues in her life.

However, there was one big issue that she chose to ignore for quite a long while. She had married a man much older than herself some ten years before. They had had no family and rather reluctantly she confessed to not wanting him to make love to her. 'He's no good at sex,' she reported, 'It's just wham, bang and that's it!' She saw her marriage as companionable and described him as an 'ineffective overgrown kid', although he had a well-paid job and some fairly rare expertise. I encouraged her to reflect further on her marriage which she did but only with reluctance. Mostly she complained of his helplessness in the house. He couldn't cook, was no good at DIY, she handled all the money, he was untidy and never knew where anything was; she had to look after everything. He was, in a nutshell, 'hopeless'. As her therapist I grew steadily more impatient with these complaints, which were split off from her ability to reflect and think about the condition of her life. Then she announced that they were planning to separate and he was being very decent about it and she hoped it was not too late to find another partner, and with him fulfilment and happiness and even, perhaps, a child.

At this point I began to feel concerned for her. My feeling was that if she left this marriage, without recognising the elements of repetition that existed within it, she might easily repeat the whole experience again with another 'hopeless' man whom she would end up treating like a 'kid'. She couldn't see that her present life experience re-called her life as a hopeless child, helpless, of 'no use to anyone' as her mother had put it.

The links with her mother and father and her own disparagement as a child were glaringly obvious to me, but for a long time she stubbornly refused to see the connections with any degree of insight. If she began to approach the material she would push herself off course, as it were, with a bit of black comedy at her own expense. I found this quite seductive and often felt that this was merely a preliminary to engaging with the past, in an insightful and deeply regretful way. But it was not so – usually the joke was abandoned and she would stride off in another direction. Although in this chapter I advocate the making of connections as if it were an easy and natural thing to do, the reality, however, is very different. We defend ourselves against knowledge, especially the kind that would really challenge us in the situation of our day-to-day lives. We settle for the status quo, believing that change is either impossible or too painful to achieve. The cost is often seen as too much to pay. This, of course, can be an illusion. Another illusion is, however, that we persuade ourselves that we have changed.

It is not the job of a psychotherapist to tell a client how to live. We have all struggled with the desire to do so in certain circumstances, such as when a client is threatened, as Jane was, with further calamity if they blindly go into the future not seeing or hearing themselves moving into a sterile repetition of the past. I suppose our primary task is to help clients find understanding in the pattern of their lives and to use this knowledge to try to shape a better future which they determine for themselves. A difficult task but one not impossible to achieve.

Belief

Listening to an edition of the *Moral Maze* on BBC Radio 4, I heard a number of religious people talking about the importance of 'faith'. Faith usually implies attachment to a system of religious belief and sometime to an iconic figure within that belief system. Of course, there are non-religious faiths but these are rarely discussed on the radio, and our Judeo-Christian culture still holds sway over much that is broadcast in the country on radio and television. This is less so in newspapers and journals, where there is less establishment influence, and journalists have a freer hand. However, there was one scientist in the *Moral Maze* discussion, a bright woman, who declared herself to be a rationalist, not an atheist or agnostic, but one atttached to the power of reason. I was interested in what she had to say. In psychotherapy we know rationality can be a poor guide and master, ousting, as it often does, the significance of emotion. This woman had a rather different stance. She claimed that for herself 'belief' was a major feature of her moral code. In discussing the legality of the war in Iraq, she 'believed' our action in attacking the country was fundamentally 'morally wrong' and she stood by this 'belief, not being persuaded otherwise by the arguments of lawyers. The religious response in the programme was muted and ambiguous. She was asserting that morality is not in the possession of religion. I noticed that her avowed value, in this instance, was enacted (Clarkson, 2000) and she had the power to influence others because of her commitment to her 'beliefs'. Her belief system gave her the power of judgement and she could work out where she stood on a whole range of issues.

Psychotherapists have, as a first principle, to acknowledge and own their own belief systems, staying alert to their influence in the transference relationship. It is important to realize that the very process of training that psychotherapists and counsellors go through is value laden. We tend to emerge from such training carrying a burden of 'belief', which influences each individual therapist in both his professional and private life (see Scecsody, 1990). The dynamics of such a situation are complicated. It can be assumed that every trainee in therapy brings to the training a personal system of 'belief' (however, this does not need to be 'religious' to be effective and powerful). These beliefs are moderated in relation to the culture of therapy, and this power-ful mix is brought into the therapy room and expressed in the therapeutic relationships. These acquired moral and ethical beliefs of childhood and adolescence are then overlaid with the ethics of therapy. Some psychoanalysts would argue that their training therapy deals with such complexities, and that they can then emerge free of psychological, moral or ethical confusion. I must admit that I am somewhat sceptical about this claim.

In recent years various psychotherapy institutes have produced ethical guidelines to which accredited therapists are expected to adhere. However a quick trawl through the more traditional psychoanalytic literature displays an absence of the terms 'ethical' or 'values' in their indexes. As I write there is a debate as to the need for government control over the registration of therapists. The argument for this is largely based on the idea of protecting the public from bad practice. Frankly, I am very doubtful that this can be achieved by a rigid registration system. There seems to be a great deal of anxious discussion as to whether therapy is seen as an all-powerful good or, equally, a deadly activity. I do not believe that registration will resolve such arguments. On the contrary I believe, along with such distinguished thinkers as Richard House (2003), that as psychotherapists we need to approach the registration and the professionalisation of psychotherapy and counselling with great caution, as it might well be an open door leading to stifling bureaucratic and institu-tional definition of what, in reality, needs to proceed as a free, enquiring and creative interpersonal journey of discovery. Richard House's recent book, *Therapy Beyond Modernity* (2003), offers an excellent bibliography of critical texts related to this issue.

Moral Issues

Many clients come to us with moral dilemmas. Some of these dilemmas arise from their own feelings of guilt, which may or may not be deserved. Psychological guilt often confuses our rational response to our social and individual relationships and, as a result, we complain that we do not know what to believe and, consequently, we do not know how to act (see, for example,

Phillips, 1994). Freud was quite clear on this. He did not entertain the idea of therapy providing proper moral guidance and he attempted to disassociate the anxiety of psychologically felt guilt from that of moral uncertainty. On the other hand, the late Nina Coltart took a more contemporary view in her book *Slouching Towards Bethlehem* (1992), when she argued that psychoanalytic therapy was attached to moral persuasion and that it advances ideas that are clearly moral in character. I am convinced that the recent emerging activity of counselling admits to the same position despite its apparent attachment to 'unconditional acceptance' as a principle precept in its practice. On the surface, the advocacy of 'unconditional acceptance' seems incontrovertible. As an ideal it is, of course, not original. Much the same has been attributed to the teaching of Christ. The phrase 'Love thy enemies' trots off the tongue easily enough. The reality of everyday human life tends, however, to throw up deep doubt about our human capacity to attain such a state of blissful acceptance of others. It seems that the psychoanalytical position of recognition of our total fallibility as humans is a safer place to occupy, even when it finds itself entangled with what Phillips describes as traditions that are seen as good, in some immutable way (Phillips, 1994). A client attempting to address moral issues within an emotional context will often challenge these so-called traditions, and then the therapist can be left struggling to reconcile the client's values with her own.

Example

I met Charles some twenty years ago, and he was the first gay man I worked with. Indeed, he was one of the most difficult clients I ever worked with. He had come from a psychotic breakdown to me for therapy from a background of homosexual activity on an international scale. Aids was just beginning to loom on the horizon of medical concern. It was referred to casually as the 'gay plague'. I felt reasonably confident that I could handle most gay issues without prejudice. I was rather flattered, too, that a professor of psychiatry (who had arranged lithium therapy for this client) had recommended me to the client for psychotherapy. The formal diagnosis was that he had suffered an acute

manic–depressive episode leading to a full-blown psychotic expe-
rience whilst attending a conference abroad. It was essential for
him to find secure, entirely confidential, therapy and he did not
trust the NHS to provide such cover. He was probably right in this
surmise.

The critical issue for him was his covert homosexuality, which
took the form of serial rent-boy partners in the UK as well as visits
to massage and bath parlours on the west coast of America and
in Hong Kong. There were good reasons to be concerned about
possible AIDS – his sex had often been unprotected anal sex with
him as the recipient and the provider. At this point no HIV pres-
ence had been discovered.

What happened in therapy came as something of a surprise to
me and a challenge to my own beliefs, emotional values and
moral stances. Charles was married with two small children, both
girls. He loved them deeply and loved his wife, enjoying sexual
relations with her. In effect, he was bi-sexual. He realised that she
was at risk of infection too, arising from his promiscuity as a gay
man of which she was quite ignorant.

It quickly became apparent to me that I had to deal with my
own strong feelings about the nature of intimate relations
between men and women, men and men, and women and
women. Charles simply objectified his sexual partners, with the
exception of his wife, as if they had no presence as fully human
beings. These casual couplings were regarded as entirely instinc-
tual, his 'id' ruled supreme in this respect, and he split off all his
normal moral feelings, evidenced in his marital partnership, to
fulfil these extremely primitive drives. In some respects he did not
identify himself as a member of the gay community. Indeed, he
pushed away any sense of commitment in his homosexual behav-
iour, and saw himself as a very successful businessman, married,
with a family, and with all the appearance of bourgeois
respectability. But the psychotic episode had happened and this
could not be denied. I found my defences challenged. Parts of me
protested against this inhuman sexual behaviour and I some-
times felt revolted by his apparent psychopathic attitude towards
some of his erstwhile partners. I could not deny that I am a moral
creature, the product of a moral culture, and these positions were
constantly being challenged within the transference relationship.
It was there in the transference that the difficulty surfaced. I

could not distance myself, as a psychologist might, in working with a deeply perverted sex offender. Charles admired me and compared his father to me disparagingly. We worked together for about three years and the final stage was when his wife came for conjoint therapy to face the issues of potential HIV infection, after hearing him confess over a period of some months to his sexual behaviour. She turned out to be a remarkable woman. I was much relieved at what seemed a reasonable closure of our relationship.

Of course, it could be argued that I should not have accepted the referral in the first place. Indeed, I have an introductory position in therapy with new clients where it is stressed that the assessment between us is two-way, and just as they may find I am not the therapist for them, I too can close the procedure. But in this instance I did not. At a later stage in my practice, when I had more confidence in my own judgement, I was better able to withdraw sometimes from a potential therapeutic contract. Indeed as a psychodramatist, in a psychiatric hospital where I worked occasionally, I nearly experienced the trauma and shame of fainting in an opening moment of a psychodrama, whilst confronting extremely violent, sadistic material with a patient (Feasey, 2001). I was 'rescued' by a sensitive and very capable co-therapist, who picked up the stress I was feeling at that moment, and who quietly and firmly closed the session. I felt somewhat reassured when I read an account of Freud fainting in the company of colleagues on his trip to America. It is well to remember we are all human.

Action

One of the most irritating things I came across when working in a large mental hospital was to hear medical staff dismissing the behaviour of patients as 'acting out' when they meant 'acting up'. The behaviour was identified as 'bad'. Sometimes the 'bad behaviour' took the form of opposition to those in authority or to those who patronised the patients. Sometimes it was addressed to staff who genuinely strove to be therapeutic, taking the form of rejection and challenge. The staff were sorely tested but the better informed of them recognised the meaning of the behaviour and worked through it, to the benefit of their patients. The action or behaviour was always coloured with institutional response. Sometimes the results were very bad as, occasionally, the response of the medical staff was also to 'act'. For example, I know of a therapy group held in a hospital, which was regularly made 'homeless', because the nurses in the acute admissions sector thought it a self-indulgent waste of time. The group would gather in their allocated room only to be turned out on the orders of a charge nurse when the room was required 'for other purposes'. The group therapist was in despair and struggled hopelessly with the clinic staff in an attempt to protect his patient group from such marginalisation and petty persecution. The irony here is, of course, that the staff were 'acting up' and 'acting out' without thought, proper judgement or insight. The term 'acting out' should, in my view, be regarded as a form of communication – something is being said by this behaviour that the patient has been unable to express in a less challenging form. So the therapist has to look for meaning in the behaviour. Trying as it may be, anti-social behaviour (or behaviour that challenges the good regard of the therapist) is invariably full of meaning that needs to be addressed. Sometimes, of course, when working privately, the opportunity to probe the meaning of this behaviour is lost when the client simply walks away from therapy. In this instance the therapist has to tolerate the frustration and anger that is likely to arise within them, and seek to understand the significance of the client's gesture.

Example

Elizabeth, a remarkably beautiful young woman, came to me for therapy. She came from a very wealthy family, successful industrialists well known locally for their cultural and charitable interests. She appeared well balanced; she was a graduate in Economics, engaged to be married to a presentable, able young man with excellent prospects. On the surface, everything seemed perfect. But there was a 'but', and she struggled with this qualifier every time she approached the subject of her forthcoming marriage. She lived with her parents in a large modern flat within an impressive and admired landscape development, the subject of some local architectural admiration. Our work was focused, after the initial exploration, on her development from childhood, through adolescence and young adulthood, with special reference to her relationship with her adoring patients. She had never left home. She had gone to a local university although she had been offered a place at Cambridge. We were beginning to get quite deep into the work when, unaccountably, she did not turn up for her regular weekly appointment. I was puzzled and waited for an explanatory phonecall. There was none. I waited a fortnight. It is my practice to give a client space to respond to such an obvious breach of our therapeutic contract. Nothing came. I thought perhaps she might write to me, but there was nothing. I began to grow angry and at this point I realised I must do two things.

First, I must try to understand this absence in relation to the work we were engaged in, and then, secondly, I had to act. The understanding that occurred to me was that she had looked at family relationships with great difficulty, and at the centre of her difficulty was the anxiety she felt about her father's relationship with her mother. She suspected him of infidelity. She fantasised that her mother had abandoned a sexual life with her father many years before. She felt as if she was held between them, keeping them apart and, at the same time, holding them together. Such was my interpretation of somewhat incoherent material. Why had she abandoned me in this way? Without her being present everything was speculation but I felt her departure was firmly associated with her sense of being bound to her parents, at the same time being pledged to her boyfriend.

I wrote her a friendly letter acknowledging that she may have been experiencing some difficulty in the therapeutic relationship. I gently urged her to return and address any issue that might exist that impelled her to leave without notice or explanation. I also sent her an invoice. A month passed, she did not respond. I sent a brief note with another invoice. No response. At that point I abandoned any further effort to elicit a response. I felt wounded, not desperately, but sufficiently to disturb my usual equanimity as a therapist. I had, of course, suffered a financial loss as well.

When thought leads to action then interpretation becomes vital to follow the meaning of what is being enacted. In this sense it is like a play. A night at the theatre finds the audience closely following the actions of the characters and, for the most part, unconsciously interpreting their motivation and the possible consequences of their actions. In the example above, the actions of both of us, both client and therapist, are open to interpretation and I imagine readers might well think to themselves that in such a circumstance they might have behaved differently.

11 Intimacy and the Limits of Therapy

The word 'therapy' implies some sort of distress has taken place, either physical or mental. We go to the doctor when we are physically distressed in order to be cured, if a cure is possible. Sometimes, of course, it is not. Fortunately, we can usually expect there will be an alleviation of distress, in whatever form it expresses itself, as a result of a visit to the doctor. In the past a visit to a psychotherapist was seen as a way of obtaining a 'cure' for some forms of mental distress. Today, however, it is rare for the term 'cure' to appear in the index of psychotherapy books. So what is the therapist actually trying to achieve? This question must be asked – otherwise what is the point of the activity?

Freud answered the question in what might be seen as a somewhat cautious way. He talked about alleviating 'misery' in favour of ordinary human unhappiness: he saw the 'normal' human state as being a state of unhappiness. In his *Five Lectures on Psychoanalysis* (1995) he ends the series by spelling out what might be accomplished by a successful analysis. At this stage of his reasoning Freud was still clearly thinking of analysis as a therapeutic procedure, and the idea of a 'cure' for emotional and mental distress was at the forefront of his mind. The first claim he made on its behalf was that good and sensible rationality will overcome irrational destructive unconscious impulses. The second claim was that by revealing the unconscious nature of repression and facing the nature of the instinctual repressed material, the client may be able to use the energy exposed in a non-neurotic manner (e.g. by sublimation). The third claim was directly concerned with the desire for proper sexual expression that has been denied to the client by a combination of neurotic inhibitions and the cultural censorship of society at large (which, Freud believed, was essentially anxious and repressive). Psychoanalysis was seen as a proper route for the client to follow in order to gain a measure of personal sexual fulfilment. However, given Freud's statement, that to be 'normal' was to be 'unhappy', it might be thought he was not a very optimistic person. Whilst talking to a client this morning and addressing his state of mind, the client remarked that, whilst not feeling neurotic, he did feel in a state of angst. I reflected that, given the times we live in, it was not at all surprising that he should be feeling this way. In this instance he was a citizen seriously concerned about the social tensions apparent not only in his own immediate community, but in British society as a whole as it struggles with issues of war and peace in a time of intense international unease. The concept of 'terrorism' that is so frequently thrust upon us – vague and imprecise and sometimes inaccurate as it may be – has a psychological presence that can operate at the deepest level of anxiety in the human psyche. In my view the terms 'terror' and 'terrorist' should be used far more cautiously.

Not all therapists and counsellors today would embrace these fundamental ideas of Freud. However, most therapists will recognise the significance of these ideas in our own time. Freud did *not* advocate a sickness model followed by a cure model, and in my view this is the most positive inheritance of modern psychotherapy. As therapists we do not have to embrace a model of medical sickness in order to justify our existence. Rather, Freud seems to have been suggesting a mixture of adjustment and accommodation, through the process of what is essentially a form of education, whereby the client comes to realise her disposition and the paths that she has led in her life journey, both at an unconscious and conscious level. A journey that may continue, albeit with difficulty, and perhaps be changed sufficiently to satisfy her desire for a good life, and lead without harm to herself or others. To work and to love; is this too much to ask?

My use of the word 'accommodating' follows on from what I have written so far. The *Pocket Oxford Dictionary* suggests various meanings for this, including, among others, the idea of 'adjustment', 'adaptation', and 'a settlement and compromise'. It is likely that most therapists and counsellors from the many different disciplines would find these suggestions acceptable in relation to the work they do. I find them reassuring. The thought of 'wiping the slate clean' emotionally and socially seems to me both undesirable and unattainable. From this it can be reasonably deduced that the process of therapy is likely to be explorative, investigative and rather slow, probably requiring some time to pass before benefit is felt. In this respect I have to part company with those who advocate quick solutions and behavioural change in a matter of weeks. That does not mean there is no place for short interventions in human affairs as these might sometimes prove beneficial. For instance, we all use our friends to 'get things off our chest' and we all benefit from sensible and well-informed advice from different sources. However, it is unlikely that there will be only benefit if the thing 'on our chest' is deeply embedded in a neurotic personal disposition or attitude, which is mainly influenced by unconscious processes. Here, in this case, the best way to achieve an effective therapeutic outcome is where, following the working through, there is a form of dynamic accommodation with the individual's past and psychological experience. This is then reflected in social experience, especially in our relationship with others about us. I use the term 'dynamic' here (implying 'movement'), for much of a psychological journey consists of movement within the mind towards and away from personal experience, both individual and social. The following example may provide a simple example of such a journey.

Example

> Andrew is fond of the sun and fond of travel, especially to faraway places where tourists are rare. He is also attempting to 'leave' a long-standing marriage, which for about 10 years has been sexually and socially moribund. Given that he is only 40 years old it seems reasonable to at least attempt a separation and divorce. His wife is more or less in agreement with his aims but does nothing to actively support them. He is frustrated because every time it begins to look as if they will achieve a mutually agreeable separation, by him leaving and finding somewhere else to live, things (or events as he would put it) go wrong. The separation does not take place and on they go together until a holiday is proposed and off they go to some remote and potentially dangerous part of the globe. His wife is an expert organiser of travel and takes control of the transport and route planning. He follows on. His only condition being there must be sunshine and very hot sun at that.

The plans to separate and divorce are abandoned temporarily and do not emerge again for some months after their return to this country. The project, 'separation', starts again and moves forward until something crops up – it may be financial, practical issues of accommodation and possession, concern about health etc. – when the plans stall again. Another expedition is planned and for the time being the issues of leaving one another are postponed.

Andrew finds many practical reasons to explain this repetitive behaviour. He calls himself a practical man. He tends to produce a mass of triviality in the therapy sessions to explain the situation, and even to excuse the failure they both experience, as if I am a sort of judge rather than a potential interpreter/traveller. However, it is clear that there is no proper dynamic in their lives that could lead to effective change and enable them to move forward in their lives separate from one another. They are in a kind of loop. My task as a therapist is to try to enable my client to move freely back and forward in his appraisal of his emotional and social life, past, present and potential future, in order to understand and negotiate with the influences that bind him so closely to the status quo. Whether he can do this on his own, in individual therapy with me, or whether he might manage it better in couples therapy remains to be seen. As yet he seems unable to recognise or appreciate the paradox of his lengthy journeys in far-flung places, places where they are bound together in mutual support in-order to survive both real and imagined hazards. This state of affairs always seem to bring him back to where he began, with nothing changed. I may have to refer him forward to a couples therapist I know, who has a good reputation. The loop needs to be broken.

So is change possible? The problem inherent in this question is how to define the manner of change. Of course a house can be sold and another one bought. Moving house is sometimes seen as a solution to recurrent difficulties – here, change is brought about, but is it the right form of change? As it happens, my client had already tried this option but fell at the first hurdle of real estate difficulty. With some persistent effort, which itself requires a degree of emotional energy and stability, it is possible to change an address. But in more meaningful terms has anything actually changed, anything to the extent that feelings is satisfied and contentment experienced in the new situation? Is it ever possible to look back at an unhappy time of our life, and now feel a sense of pleasure at having 'moved on'?

Many critics (see, for example, Jeffrey Masson, 1992) have grown impatient with psychoanalysis because it is alleged that whatever reality change occurs, the client is always still left wriggling on the hook of their own neurosis. More recent psychotherapeutic views, particularly those in the field of counselling, take a more optimistic view (see, for example, Rogers, 1967). This appeals to a blend of rationality and emotional expression/adjustment, accompanied by insight, to bring about positive change. Of course, this idea has a strong appeal and there has been a remarkable growth in the field of counselling training in the last ten years. Today it is common for all kinds of institutions to provide counselling support to its members. This has been noted by some as a positive development in society, whereby even supposedly remote employers now recognise their duty to exercise care towards their employees. On the other hand, critics such as House (2003) perceive the growth of profession-based psychotherapies, whatever their declared methods and intents, as having one thing in common: subordinating the 'client' to mechanisms of emotional and social control. Older readers who recall seeing the brilliant American musical *West Side Story* will remember the parodying of psychological therapy, in the circumstances of criminality, where a policeman sings, 'This guy doesn't need a social worker, he needs a year in the "pen".'

Alongside of this development has grown a vast literature of self-help and 'personal-growth' material. Our newspapers and magazines, radio and, most potently, television services abound with programmes where people and their personal problems are held up for psychotherapeutic scrutiny by the world. Sometimes the media is benign and poses as therapeutic, but sometimes it indulges in thinly disguised sadism, as the frailties of human nature are exposed for what they often are, foolish and self-regarding. Those of us who follow such media revelations with keen interest contribute towards the masochistic desires of the participants and legitimise the sadistic forces working in the public communication systems. The situation seems paradoxical. The more we as individuals in society strive for good mental health, whatever that may mean, the more we become patholo-gised by the institutions of care and communication around us. There is a danger that our pursuit of enlightenment and self-development will merely lead to discontent and disillusion.

Set against this is the concept of the 'therapeutic alliance'. From a relational point of view the concept of this alliance is naturally based on an assumption of mutual respect and openness concerning the therapeutic work that is embedded in the contract. In other words, the client is not there to be 'treated' by the activity of the therapist or the therapeutic organisational prac-tice of a clinic or hospital. The relationship should not be hierar-chical, based upon some supposed superiority of the insights and understanding of the therapist or counsellor. On the contrary, the client is in the relationship to engage in an alliance with the therapist towards a given and agreed aim. This aim, whilst not specific in what is sometimes described as behavioural outcomes, is associated with the desire of the client to understand and relate creatively to the nature of herself – in other words, to 'be' and to know about the nature of her 'being' (Buber, 1970).

Petruska Clarkson (2000) writes very sensibly about this aspect of therapy and points out that the alliance is not a perfect construct. It is, she says, a human activity subject to all the diffi-culties that may arise between persons, whatever their feelings about one another, and the construct of their relationship (Clarkson, 2000, p. 53). Professionals in relationship with clients, whilst guarding against distortions in the therapeutic relation-ship, cannot claim any exemption from disturbing and distorting elements. However, Clarkson suggests, the value of a working relationship is that it always offers a reparative aspect, which can address such malfunctioning experiences. The best situation seems to be that of intimacy between strangers, an idea expressed included in the sub-title of this book, where the intention is entirely therapeutic and when the therapist subordinates self-interest to the needs of her client.

Unfortunately, there is an increasing demand for a different kind of relationship, one where the focus is not upon a therapeu-tic relationship but on the identification and realisation of behav-ioural aims within a short time scale. The problem with short-term therapy or counselling is that it rarely allows the necessary time for a substantial healing relationship to be established, stabilised and utilised in an alliance of therapy. It may afford some temporary relief from anxiety and provide some insight, but the actual working through, which is possible in a powerful alliance, is denied. Unfortunately, owing to for financial and management constraints, patients entering the NHS for therapy often find themselves consigned to short-term work. Usually they are not in a position to challenge this arrangement or know how to judge its value in relation to their needs.

A further problem is the 'academicism' (House, 2003) of much therapy training where the culture of 'education' impinges on the therapeutic process. In recent years educationists have become enchanted with the notion of learning outcomes, and our unfortunate children and students are now often burdened with measurements of their learning process, based upon the notion of specific measurable knowledge outcomes. It is not surprising then that clients too may be subject to such a scrutiny. Some therapists and agencies will impose an idea of desired outcome upon their needy clients, especially an outcome that is objective and measurable. When this occurs, many of the first principles of psychotherapy are marginalised or abandoned altogether. The key to good therapy is clear. Therapy is based upon a trusting exploration, led by the client into the condition of her life, in association with a person, the therapist, who joins the exploration without any preconceived ideas about the destiny that is to be pursued. A moment usually occurs in therapy when the client decides upon the nature of the journey she is to make beyond therapy and she will pursue that journey. She may, indeed, decide to accommodate the present reality of her life, only making marginal changes in her behaviour in relation to her living relationships and social position, to order to achieve her personal aims. That is her right.

Example

Harry, aged 53, tall, good looking, intelligent, although not especially well educated, married with three sons, presented himself for therapy after attending a seminar I had given at an Institute of Psychotherapy on the subject of the dynamics of family life. I recalled him from the seminar, remembering his keen interest in the topic, making contributions, although cautiously put, clearly emerging from his own family life. He was a social worker accustomed to dealing with all the complexities of family disorder in the work with his clients who, for the most part, were very poor, lacking decent housing, having no personal transport and usually treated with disdain by those around them.

When he rang up I assumed he was looking for an opportunity to advance his training and possibly enrol at the Institute for full training in psychodynamic therapy, which is offered to many social workers and medical personnel. But I was wrong. He smiled at me warmly as he entered the room and spoke of enjoying my seminar and then suddenly, with a rather sad grin, he said, 'It's a question of healer heal thyself, as far as I am concerned.' I was immediately intrigued although not entirely surprised. Thinking back to the seminar I recalled his good-humoured exasperation when describing the wayward, lazy behaviour of young women, emerging from adolescence into maturity. At the same time he had admitted being very attracted by them and happy when they appeared to acknowledge his sexuality.

In this initial meeting I did not particularly follow his self-deprecating approach. I spoke of other things to him. I talked about my approach to therapy, discussed a simple contract with him, pointed out that I may not be the best person for him to approach but I could and would help him to find another should the need arise. We discussed money and frequency of attendance. He was rather shocked when I told him he would have to attend once a week, every week, until the work, as far as he and hopefully I was concerned, was finished. I think he had thought a monthly meeting would be enough. He left to think things over and returned the following week keen to make a start. His final concern was the issue of confidentiality. He was terrified that his colleagues would think of him as a 'nutter in therapy'. I assured him that my confidentiality could be trusted and was absolute but he had his family to think of. That was enough to prompt him to focus upon his decision to come to me and what the consequences may be.

The work went on for two years. Sometimes he appeared to be stuck, fearful of the possibilities that emerged as he addressed his sexless marriage, the Oedipal collusion of his sons and his own *occasional infidelities. It was a comfort and a trial to him that again and again he was forced to take on the responsibility for his own life, its colour, tone, ambiguities, denials, frustrations and future possibilities. I was not going to be his mentor, his guide, and certainly not, to quote Wilde, provide a model of 'An ideal husband'! To make adjustments he needed to bring enrichment to his life, albeit within a limited spectrum. This was not easy and he needed a fairly long period of assimilative closure to encounter the experience of change and to enact it in a meaningful manner. The greater part was to accept that his wife was not going to change significantly in her relationship to him, despite his efforts to bring change into the relationship.*

Along with this he set out to cope with the feelings of guilt that arose in him when he attempted to relieve sexual tension either through flirtation, and sometimes direct experience of sexual contact, or alternatively through masturbation accompanied by fantasy. In this respect he found the book by Nancy Friday, My Secret Garden *(1975), very helpful and enlightening. Like a lot of middle-class, middle-aged men of his age and time he had had very little premarital sexual experience and his infidelities had been heavily tinged with feelings of shame. There had been no sex education available as he was growing up and his parents shunned the topic. During his training for social work he had been in a training group but intimate subjects had been avoided and the focus had been on the relationship with clients rather than their own personal anxieties. Open discussion of personal sexual tension had been discouraged by the culture of the group and the interventions of the therapist. Only when discussing ethical issues was the fear of sexual contact with clients ever discussed, and then it was limited to the professional consequences of improper use of power, disgrace and loss of status.*

It is interesting, too, that despite an earlier emphasis upon sexual anxiety as a root cause of neurotic disorder, the contemporary world of therapy and counselling seems to have moved its emphasis to safer ground. The current emphasis upon the need for spiritual growth may restrain the client from opening herself to admission of deeply felt and experienced sexual desires and taboos. It is as if the two positions are seen to be mutually incompatible. The only group I am aware of that seems to have given priority to addressing powerful sexual issues is the gay community, which has had to work through the trauma of the AIDs crisis.

For the therapist much of the above discussion is material for supervision, and in the earlier chapters of this book I have mentioned and discussed the process of psychotherapy supervision. Classical psychoanalysis, from which so much of the culture of psychotherapy and counselling derives, is sometimes teased by informed critics for encouraging what has been seen as the 'fleas upon the back of fleas' syndrome. The suggestion is that there are humble armies of practitioners at the coal face actually working with distressed and needy clients and behind them are the supervisors, who only ever see a few actual clients, and beyond them are the trainers who see even fewer. All these people are economically dependent upon the clients, but the clients rarely, if ever, see them. As somebody once described the situation:

Well, who supervises the supervisors and who supervises them? As for the trainers, well perhaps they have a vague and lofty world of supervision that is beyond the conception of the therapists at the coal face.

And so it goes on. I will go no further with this conundrum but place it back into a context where it can be discussed relevantly. I always give assurances of confidentiality to my clients, and did so to the man mentioned in the example above. However, the truth is that I shall reveal information about him to a supervisor, just as my supervisees reveal confidential material to me. I also give assurances concerning confidentiality to my supervisees. Therapists and counsellors give all of these assurances in good faith. Indeed, it is regarded as a principle value of therapy and counselling that we offer such reassurances. The reality, however, is a little different. If challenged by a court or by a policeman investigating a crime, or an employer concerning a misdemeanor, where would we stand then? Fortunately I have never had to face that dilemma.

In group psychotherapy, whatever its character or culture and practice, there can be no such thing as confidentiality for the group members. They might give each other reassurances towards that end, but the reality is that information, even gossip, will leak out from such a milieu. Group therapists often go for group supervision, and once again one must be sceptical as to its inviolability as far as confidentiality is concerned. The notion of confidentiality is based, I believe, on fear. It is obviously related to the Catholic practice of confession where shameful sins are declared to the priest who then relieves the confessor of sin, through forgiveness, who then goes away 'cleansed'. These sins are told to the priest who is bound by oath not to reveal them to anyone else. Although therapists and counsellors are not bound by any such official oath, they are viewed in a similar way by the principles of their profession.

Many of our clients are ashamed of the emotional material they wish to express and this shame stretches out to their relatives and friends from whom they keep their deadly secrets. The clients find some security in the confidence of the therapy room. An example of this happened this very morning, when a young woman client decided to tell her father about her long-standing relationship with a married man. She feels she must tell her father the truth but shrinks from his judgement because, she is ashamed. The first step towards this 'confession' to her father is to reveal and discuss the situation with me, her transference father. I suit this position well as I am about the age of biological father. However, she can rely on me not to judge her morally.

I have much sympathy with the criticism made by some informed commentators, such as Richard House where, in his book *Therapy Beyond Modernity* (2003, pp. 142–6), he expresses misgivings concerning the intensity of feeling that can be brought into the therapeutic relationship through the activity of transference. However, I would argue that to suggest that all that is really required, as an alternative, is a genuine interest and friendship by the therapist towards the client, to facilitate a therapeutic experience, is to avoid facing the issues of guilt and shame I have spoken of in this book. I believe that in truth the therapist has to find a subtle and delicate blend of these two positions. I have no faith in the 'blank screen' approach and when I have encountered it as a client I have found it oppressive and inhuman. On the other hand, a therapist who, unwittingly through friendship, 'hamstrings' a client (holding her within the natural constraints of a socially determined emotional friendship) is not performing effectively or, in my view, towards the true interests of the client. Indeed, attractive as it might be to think of the relationship between client and therapist as being vested in a kind of enhanced friendship, the reality is that friends have to be won and kept and due attention has to be given to their needs. Where we fail to do this, we may lose a friend and find ourselves abandoned. I believe that the intimacy of the therapy room has be built upon more clearly defined, professionally friendly, relationships, where boundaries and commitments towards therapy are understood and respected, (even in a situation where the therapist is working at a net emotional loss). A loss because our natural desire as persons for self-gratification has to be put aside in favour of another person. The therapist has to do this consistently and throughout the therapeutic relationship. This is often too much to ask of friendship. Part of the process of accommodation (i.e. coming to terms with the self we are accepting, the idea of being and finding value in ourselves) is bound up with the experience of speaking aloud to another, in the intimacy of the therapy room, our most hidden feelings and fantasies. Although others beyond the room may have no access to this process, the client has now to live with the knowledge of revelation to another (the therapist) that which has been previously forbidden expression. There are sometimes deep anxieties concerning the revelation of formerly repressed feelings towards our intimates within the context of the therapy room The reparation of the self is bound up with this process. I believe that once the therapy has closed, the client may find the secrets need no longer be so closely guarded. In the fullness of time these old confessions may be revealed to those in relation to her, albeit newly interpreted in the light of insight and experience in the therapeutic relationship. Thus the process of reparation goes on.

I have used the expression 'intimacy in the therapy room' in the paragraph above and something similar in the sub-title of this book (where it appears as 'Intimacy between Strangers'). Some readers may feel the use of this phrase was to catch attention on the shelves of bookshops and libraries where books on therapy jostle for attention and sales. I can categorically say that this is not the intention of the title. I hope the book sells well and is read sympathetically by reviewers and readers alike, and I hope I have been describing the meaning of the phrase 'intimacy in the therapy room' adequately: Here I want to put it into the context of the phrase 'intimate relationship'.

Most therapists are now aware of the phenomenon of 'transference', which I have discussed in some detail in Chapter 2. And it is within the idea of transference that I believe the notion of 'Intimacy between Strangers' occurs in the therapy room when work is in progress. The therapy room is a privileged space. Certain rules apply to conduct within it but it also allows a great freedom to express ideas and feelings. Paradoxically, it is also a place where physical action is inhibited. At the closure of therapy both therapist and client face the prospect of separation. The therapist is best equipped to deal with the issue of the loss of this relationship. Loss it is, and therapists and counsellors alike need to acknowledge this as a fact. The closer the relationship has been – a relationship where empathy has been found, understanding has emerged, and a depth and range of emotional discovery has been experienced – the more will have to be put aside. There has to be time in therapy to move towards a parting and an end to the therapeutic process. I usually say to clients as they leave that they may feel a desire to ring me up to ask for a 'one off' consultation after the contract between us is concluded. I suggest that in this circumstance the impulse should be resisted. That is not to say that there could never again be a therapeutic meeting between us. However, I feel that there is a need for emotional space and time at this point, in which the former client can adjust to the new situation and make any necessary accommodations. Similarly, I need to place the relationship to one side in favour of the newcomers who are entering into the same position with me, and with whom I have to journey until they, too, go on their way without me. Thus the intimacy of therapy differs from a good friendship, no matter how valued that might be, and it is less than the ecstasy and abandonment of sexual engagement. It stands in a kind of hinterland where the essential elements of therapy are freedom for the client and a compelling interest from the therapist. This interest compels the therapist to stand unflinching alongside the client, whatever occurs and whatever is revealed, until the work is judged to be done.

Example

Jenny was a teacher. She taught English in a well-respected girls' grammar school in the midlands. It was a state school with a liberal academic reputation, where the pupils were encouraged to explore and find themselves through the subjects they chose to study. As a result, relationships between staff and students were often close. The staff, on the whole, were united and companionable, confident in the value of their school and its public reputation. I knew the school and was intrigued when this teacher presented herself to me as a potential client. She complained of tension and stress in her performance in the school, at not being properly valued by other teachers, at being criticised by the head teacher, who she described as an 'old blue stocking fuddy duddy'.

My client's appearance had been remarked upon in school. She resented this. She considered herself smart and attractive in appearance, if slightly unconventional in her choice of clothes. The day she came to see me she was wearing a long silk, multicoloured scarf over her black jumper, together with an ankle-length flared skirt. She certainly commanded attention. At first I was puzzled. Why had she come to me? All the matters she brought up were the day-to-day complaints that any of us might make to a friend concerning our jobs and careers. I felt there was more to come. And it did.

It was at meeting six when she launched into a long account of her feelings towards girls in the sixth form to whom she was responsible for English 'A' level teaching. Her account was low key. She did not look at me. It was as if she were holding an internal monologue, requiring nothing from me other than to listen and pay close attention. She spoke of their burgeoning sexuality, their interest in boys, especially those from a neighbouring boys' school. And then she said, 'All except one, and I think she is interested in me.' Her secret was out.

The tone of her voice expressed satisfaction and pleasure and excitement. It was at this point that she looked at me. I believe she was reading my face for a response, perhaps for approval. But for what? Approval of her courage, perhaps, in revealing a hidden world, or in my recognition of her value as a lesbian? Although she was a woman with a wide social circle she had no confidante to speak to about her sexual disposition. Later she told me that she had never met an adult lesbian at any time before in her life. Indeed, she was currently having an intense sexual relationship with a young married man she had met at an arts club, who had offered a range of sexual expression which she had never experienced before. She was very grateful to him, but she did not love him. The satisfaction was mainly of lust and fantasy gratified with a confident lover, whose only demand was secrecy in the relationship.

There was much work to be done but the first issue of her sexual identity was a discussion of her interest in the girl. Accompanying it, of course, arose conflict in relation to her duty of care towards the teenage girl concerned. Essentially she was in 'loco parentis' and this cast a deep shadow upon her feelings of attraction, together with a powerful sense of guilt in that attraction. The work went on for some years. The material led us back into her childhood, her relations with her parents and the powerful emotional and social influences that helped repress her knowledge of herself. As far as the place of friends in therapy is concerned, she confessed that she had only once opened up to a close woman friend who misinterpreted the approach and shied away from the discussion, believing that she herself might be the subject of my client's erotic interest. The transference towards me was mostly parental in nature, together with heterosexual projections confirming her essential attractiveness to others, including men. This did not prevent me from adopting an accepting 'friendly' approach to her, but the friendliness was without obligation on her part. The payment of a fee determined our 'real' relationship with each other. I was a professional man who accompanied her through therapy in a friendly manner. I was a free person who could and would listen and speak without fear of social consequences. If she was angry with me, I did not reciprocate with anger and disappointment; if she 'loved' me I did not take her into a compromising emotional or sexual relationship. I was there for her, come what may.

I have no doubt that following therapy, when she had moved substantially towards accepting her lesbian identity, she would move more confidently into adult lesbian experiences in pursuit of a long term and supportive relationship, which could be openly pursued and acknowledged by those close to her both socially and professionally. To this end she set about looking for another job in a mixed-sex comprehensive school, a school with a liberal reputation, some miles away.

Before concluding this discussion of the special nature of the therapist's role in therapy, it is worth pointing out that a client's husband, wife, mother, father, brothers or sisters, as well as other very close figures, may resent the specialness of the therapist in the client's life. They may fear disclosures about their own place in the client's life (Freud, 1995). Perhaps they imagine themselves under attack from the client, within the secrecy of the therapy room, and resent it. Sometimes in our everyday relationships with a friend we are given information that in a sense we would rather not hear, knowing that the information may well condition our response to another, who forms part of our friendship network. The therapist is relieved of this problem. The act of disclosure belongs to the client.

12 Now What? The Challenge of the End of Therapy

> *An intrepid traveller talking on the radio was asked about his feelings concerning the end of the journey. His response was immediate and confident. He stated that the end of the journey was not the point of the exercise, rather it was the journey that mattered and it was the journey that was remembered.*

As I write this final short chapter I realise how indebted I am to a client, a woman in her fifties, who is concluding six years of therapy with me. She has been a serious, entertaining and rewarding client. She has been a therapeutic figure who has rewarded me for the hours of patient work she has done in our weekly sessions. The reward has been financial, emotional and social. She has taken me on journeys into her life, both interpersonal and intrapsychic, opening up vistas of knowledge and interest for me and discovery for herself. When she leaves, as she will in a few months time, we will miss each other. At this point I am thinking about her own commentary on the task that lies ahead. She began by talking enthusiastically about a book written by Dorothy Rowe (a writer I much admire), in which Rowe had set out a view of the necessary emotional tasks that lead us into the notion of maturity (Rowe, 2001). She seized on the idea of 'responsibility'. She acknowledged her own tendencies to get caught up with the excitement of infant-driven fantasy, mostly drawing her into rather grand gestures and schemes of work. These tendencies have sometimes been undermining, taking her into unrealistic ventures with consequent great social, personal and professional loss and sometimes debilitating depression.

Her thoughts on responsibility were that, rather than imposing on herself a restrictive, conservative framework of control, behaving responsibly would enable her to accept the presence of 'infantile' and 'adult' states as conjointly operating in her life. To be responsible is to accept and acknowledge this state of being, and with insight weigh each response up, one against the other, towards finding healthy solutions. Not perfect ones but healthy responses that offer space for negotiation and change in lifestyle and accomplishment. Within an adult life there has to be room for infant pleasure and pain otherwise curiosity, play, inventiveness, creativity, imagination and all the delightful manifestations of child innocence may be impaired and sadly lost.

This therapeutic discussion accords well with my own view of the tasks that follow the close of therapy. The approach of ending throws up a number of responses in the client. The task of the therapist is to enable a working through of the process of leaving without accelerating or impeding its progress. The pace of change must reflect the therapeutic relationship between therapist and client – in other words, a relational approach is needed. There is no formula for this movement. For the client there often comes a vision of 'afterwards', of what lies in front of her when the relationship with the therapist closes. Sometimes there is a feeling near to panic. This is usually a passing, quite a normal feeling, associated with the idea of managing the self relatively alone, until it is remembered that the self is rarely alone in the sense of having no interpersonal relationships. Sometimes the feeling comes from a more profound recognition of our existential aloneness and the thought of dying. This is a different matter, and not necessarily one to be addressed in therapy exclusively. For some there will be an important spiritual dimension that needs to be respected. The interpersonal relationships that we hold in our lives usually provide a cluster of friends and relatives and colleagues that we know we can trust with a degree of personal revelation (I discussed this possibility, and its limitations, in Chapter 10). My view is that the client, when leaving, is taking responsibility for herself, and is now better equipped to sense how far the possibilities stretch in her personal relationships, in a manner that will prove productive to her in the future. That position is the product of good therapy. Certainly my client saw pretty clearly what she could expect from her social intimates and, most importantly, where and when the line of confidence would need to be drawn. In this case, the client was poised on the edge of an important professional adventure. I have found over the years that sometimes an ending precipitates discovery of new fields of endeavour to be explored. For me, becoming a therapist over twenty years ago was associated with the collapse of a large educational institution in which I had been a senior academic figure. To my surprise I was not especially dismayed by the event, although I had been a happy and contented lecturer running several degree courses. Rather, I found myself quite naturally examining my life and thinking, 'Well, what happens next?'

I turned back to consider my life-long interest in psychoanalysis and the surrounding literature. I thought of the psychoanalytic movement as a cultural movement, as in the fiction of D. H. Lawrence, as well as a clinical one. I believe that most people have these critical moments of change and movement in their lives, sometimes faced fearfully, sometimes welcomed. The client leaving therapy after sometimes years of work faces an unknown future, as we all do. Good therapy and good leaving ensures at least some degree of psychic strength to begin to address the forthcoming life to be lived.

For the therapist there is a reward in a good ending. A deep sense of satisfaction comes when watching and participating with a long-standing client who is moving away and onwards in the life journey. This may be the end of therapy for her. It may not. Therapy moves away from an act of desperation, of the desire to end pain, towards a realisation that it can be a journey of satisfaction and new discovery, leading to new knowledge of the self and, consequently, others. Frankly, I have little patience with the familiar complaint that therapy is an act of self-indulgence. It is work. It is normal for a therapist in relationship with a client to benefit from personal therapy, and this may be experienced in parallel to the work with a client. In this sense therapy is intensely social as well as individual. Paradoxically, the ending promises gain rather than loss for the client. For the therapist, however, there is a mixture of both. There may be an immediate sense of loss, especially of income for the independent therapist, but often in the longer term there is also a sense of satisfaction and gain.

At the beginning of this chapter I used the word 'change'. Many years ago I worked with a consultant psychotherapist in the NHS, and she reflected upon a particular patient who was moving out of therapy and would cease to be her patient in a matter of some weeks. The consultant turned to me and said:

The big difference in him now is that he can tolerate and embrace the experience of change in his life. When he first came to our therapeutic community not much change of any significance had happened to him for many years. He had a feeling of being stuck. So badly stuck that only a death or a cataclysmic social upheaval would end or change his life. He was waiting upon external events to release him from what he saw as the quagmire of his life. Now he feels he can motivate himself. He can choose to change his life's direction.

Obviously there is a danger that the therapist might either consciously or unconsciously try to exert a powerful influence upon the choices that are now occurring to the client, as well as decisions to be made in the future. In the case mentioned above, the biggest feature of the man's choice was, at the age of forty, to leave the home of his aging parents and set up on his own. He would then seek to retrain in a skill that would lead to a job and get him off benefits. Now obviously these changes sound admirable enough. But sometimes the changes that are set in place by departing clients suggest far more risk and may be even destructive to structures that they have held in place for a long time. This can be hard for the therapist to tolerate and there may be attempts to hold the client in therapy, to postpone separation until an acceptable change has been proposed. But acceptable to whom? A psychoanalytical therapist may well believe that she is detecting unresolved conflicts that will almost certainly become active again when the client ceases therapy. Another belief the therapist might hold is that the client is seeking a 'flight into health', or as Malan (1979) puts it, 'apparent' health. This occurs when the path of therapy appears so difficult or painful or unending that the client looks for a way out of it. Clearly, one way out is to appear to 'recover' from the original position of unhealth that brought her to therapy in the first place.

The problem here is who knows best? The therapist may be convinced of the correctness of her view, based upon her understanding of the client and the theoretical model that she is employing in her work with the client. But none of this has any testable viability. Similarly, the client may be equally convinced of her correctness in leaving therapy. So what lies ahead is problematical. Although I started this chapter on an optimistic note, the reality of the close of therapy can be very different.

Example

Jonathan arrived as always on time. He slumped in the chair in my therapy room. He gave me no eye contact or overt recognition of his own or my presence. I sat with him in silence for a short while and then, quite suddenly, the floodgates of anger and pain broke open. He began a long angry monologue: he was going to finish therapy that day; I was not right for him; I was not kind; I did not care for him; he had to find someone who cared for him; I had said all kinds of harsh things to him, which demeaned him; he knew he was better than that; he was strong enough to leave and find someone else; I didn't care for him and had told him to leave; I said he was too difficult to work with . . .

I listened to all this with a growing sense of dismay. Jonathan was a very difficult client. He had suffered gross physical and emotional abuse from his mother as a child, and his father had been largely absent, often working away from home. Jonathan had been made into the scapegoat of the family. He had not been loved or cared for. Behind him was a trail of other therapists whom had 'failed' him. Now I was about to join that group. I felt angry and dismayed. I wanted to protest at his torrent of condemnation and it took a great effort of professional will to maintain eye contact with him, to keep quiet but at the same time adopt a posture of caring concern and close attention to what he was saying. And so it went on. Tears were running down his face: these tears coming from a man who often complained he could not cry. About ten minutes went by and the flood of feeling began to ease and his body grew less tense. I had thought he might 'leave' me by simply getting up and dashing out of the house. But slowly he began to manage his feelings and modify his language towards a more introspective position. I began to talk about his need for love. I spoke of the absence of love in his mother, the absence of his father. I spoke of the futile attempts he had made to get this love from therapists, of the boundaries between us and that even this morning he would have to leave on time to make room for the next client. He listened and appeared to acknowledge my presence with him. I spoke of my real interest in him and that I thought, although the work was difficult, we could go on working together. And so it went on. He did not walk out in anger and disappointment. At the time of closure he paid me and made another appointment.

Jonathan did not leave, but there have been others who have – walking out prematurely with a host of rationalisations to support their decision. As a private therapist I have no means of detaining them, or giving more than is on offer. For me this is the worse kind of ending: inevitably I have to face myself and challenge my ability as a psychotherapist. I am 'punished' by a loss of income and sometimes I doubt if my telephone will ever ring again with another referral. I am left wondering about the departed client. I wonder how they are managing, if they have found a better therapist than me and are prospering. My fear is that they have fallen deeper into the slough of despond, and my very worse fear is of their untimely end: suicide. Such are the fantasies that all therapists have to struggle with, albeit with help from colleagues.

At closure the task for both therapist and client is simply to move ahead with hope and determination, towards, hopefully, a good future. Not perfect but good.

References

Anderson, Robin (1992) *Clinical Lectures on Klein and Bion* (London: Routledge).

Anonymous (2002) Review of *Hidden Minds: A History of the Unconscious* by Frank Tallis, *Guardian*, 9 March 2002.

Argyle, M. (1969) *Social Interaction* (London: Methuen).

Ashley, Jill (2003) 'On Being There', *British Journal of Psychotherapy*, 19:3.

Babiker, Gloria (2002) 'Relational Perspective on Shame as Expressed Through the Body', *Journal of West Midlands Institute*, 2:1.

Barnes, Bill, Ernst, Sheila and Hyde, Keith (1999) *An Introduction to Group Work* (Basingstoke: Palgrave Macmilllan).

Benson, Ophelia (2003) 'Not Much Makes Sense in Theory', *Guardian*, no. 48913.

Brown, Dennis and Peddar, Jonathan (1979) *Introduction to Psychotherapy* (London: Tavistock).

Buber, Martin (1970) *I and Thou* (Edinburgh: T. & T. Clark).

Casement, Patrick (1985) *On Learning from the Patient* (London: Tavistock).

Clark, W. Ronald (1980) *Freud: The Man and the Cause* (London: Jonathan Cape; Weidenfeld & Nicolson).

Clarke, Liam (1998) 'Back to the Present', *Changes Journal*, 16:1.

Clarkson, Petruska (2000) *The Therapeutic Relationship* (London: Whurr).

Coltart, N. (1992) *Slouching Towards Bethlehem and Other Psychoanalytic Explorations* (London: Free Association Books).

Coltart, N. (1993) *How to Survive as a Psychotherapist* (London: Sheldon Press).

Corsini, R. (ed.) (1973) *Current Psychotherapies* (Illinois: F. E. Peacock).

Coetzee, J. M. (1999) *Disgrace* (London: Martin Secker & Warburg).

Dinnerstein, Dorothy (1999) *The Mermaid and the Minataur* (London: The Other Press).

Dryden, W. (ed.) (1984) *Individual Therapy in Britain* (London: Harper & Row).

Fairbairn, W. R. D. (1952) *Psychoanalytic Studies of the Personality* (London: Tavistock).

Fast, J. (1978) *Body Language* (London: Pan Books).

Feasey, Don (1982) 'The Oedipal Aspect of Neurosis in the Treatment of Three Young Women in a Private Practice', *West Midlands Journal of Psychotherapy Journal*, 2.

Feasey, Don (1998) 'Will it or Won't it Work?', *Changes Journal*, 16:2.

Feasey, Don (2000) *Good Practice in Psychotherapy and Counselling* (London: Whurr).

Feasey, Don (2001) *Good Practice in Psychodrama: An Analytic Perspective* (London: Whurr).

Feasey, Don (2002a) 'Money . . . for What it is Worth', *Journal of Critical Psychology, Counselling and Psychotherapy*, 2:3.

Feasey, Don (2002b) Letter, *West Midlands Jounal of Psychotherapy*, 21.

Feasey, Don (2002c) *Good Practice in Supervision* (London: Whurr).

Flanagan, Helen (2003) 'Where the Wild Things Are', *West Midlands Institute of Psychotherapy Journal*, 22:3.

Folland, Mark (1994) 'On Silence in Psychotherapy', unpublished dissertation, Manchester University.

Foulkes, S. H. (1957) *Group Psychotherapy* (London: Pelican Books).

Freud, S. (1957) *The Interpretation of Dreams* (London: Pelican edition, Penguin Books).

Freud, S. (1962) *Two Short Accounts of Psychoanalysis* (Harmondsworth: Penguin).

Freud, S. (1973) *Introductory Lectures on Psychoanalysis* (London: Penguin Freud Library).

Freud, S. (1974) *The Standard Edition of the Complete Psychological Works of Sigmund Freud*, 24 vols, ed. James Strachey and Anna Freud (London: Hogarth Press).

Freud, S. (1975) *The Complete Letters of Sigmund Freud to Wilhelm Fiess, 1807–1904*, ed. J. H. Masson (London: Belknap Press, Harvard University Press).

Freud, S. (1995a) *The Libido Theory and Narcissism in Introductory Lectures on Psychoanalysis* (London: Penguin).

Freud, S. (1995b) *Five Lectures on Psychoanalysis* (London: Penguin).

Freud, S. and Breuer, J. (1974) *Studies on Hysteria* (London: Pelican edition. Penguin Books).

Friday, Nancy (1975) *My Secret Garden* (London: Arrow Books).

Fromm-Reichman, Freda (1950) *Principles of Intensive Psychotherapy* (Chicago: Chicago University Press).

Goldie, Lawrence (1989) 'Psychoanalysis in the NHS General Hospital', *London Psychoanalytic Psychotherapy*, 1:2.

Gorer, G. (1966) *Psychoanalysis Observed* (London: Penguin Books).

Guntripp, H. (1968) *Schizoid Phenomena, Object Relations and the Self* (London: Hogarth Press).

Heller, Joseph (1994) *Catch-22* (New York: Vintage).

Holmes, P. and Karp, M. (1991) *Psychodrama, Inspiration and Technique* (London: Routledge).

House, R. (2003) *Therapy Beyond Modernity: Deconstructing and Transcending Profession-Centred Therapy* (London: Karnac).

Humphreys, Nicolas (2003) 'Fascination and its Relation to Ego-Self States', *British Journal of Psychotherapy*, 20:1.

Jacobs, Michael (1992) *Sigmund Freud* (London: Sage Publications).

Jennings, S. (1973) *Models of Practice in Dramatherapy* (London: Routledge).

Jones, Ernest (1982) *Sigmund Freud: His Life and Work* (London: Penguin).

Jung, Carl (1975) *Memories, Dreams, Reflections* (London: Fontana Library Theology and Philosophy).

Jung, Carl (1978) *Man and His Symbols* (London: Pan Books).

Klein, M. (1932) *The Psychoanalysis of Children* (London: Hogarth Press).

Klein, M. (1975) *Envy and Gratitude and Other Works* (New York: Delacourt).

Kovel, Joel (1978) *A Complete Guide to Therapy* (London: Pelican Books).

Levi, Primo (1981) *If this is a Man* (London: Abacus Books).

Luepnitz, Ann Deborah (2003) *Schopenhauer's Porcupines* (New York: Basic Books).

Malan, H. D. (1979) *Individual Psychotherapy and the Science of Psychodynamics* (London: Butterworth).

Malcolm, Janet (1981) *Psychoanalysis: The Impossible Profession* (London: Picador).

Marzillier, John (1995) 'Some Reflections on the Psychology of Money', *Changes Journal*, 14:2.

Masson, J. M. (1992) 'The Tyranny of Psychotherapy', in W. Dryden and C. Feltham (eds), *Psychotherapy and its Discontents* (Buckingham: Open University Press).

Masson, Jeffrey (1992) *Final Analysis* (London: Fontana).

Masters, W. H. and Johnson. V. E. (1985) *Human Sexual Inadequacy* (New York: Lippincott, William and Wilkins).

McGuire, William and McGlashan, Alan (1974) *The Freud/Jung Letters* (London: Picador).

Meador, B. D. and Rogers, C. (1972) 'Client-Centred Therapy', in R. Corsisini (ed.), *Current Psychotherapies* (Illinois: F. E. Peacock).

Mitchell, J. (1976) *Psychoanalysis and Women* (Harmondsworth: Pelican Books).

Mitchell, S. A. (1988) *Relational Concepts* (Cambridge, MA: Harvard University Press).

Mitchell, S. A. (1995) *Hope and Dread in Psychoanalysis* (New York: Basic Books).

Moloney, Paul (2001) 'Are We Allowed to Disagree', *The Critical Journal of Psychology, Counselling and Psychotherapy*, 1:2.

Moreno, J. L. (1923) *Theatre of Spontaneity* (New York: Beacon Books).

Newnes, Craig, Holmes, Guy and Dunn, Cailzie (1999) *This is Madness* (Ross-on-Wye: PCCS Books).

Orbach, Susie (1999) *The Impossibility of Sex* (London: Penguin Books).

Orbach, Susie (2003) 'There is No Such Thing as a Body', Part 1, *British Journal of Psychotherapy*, 20:1.

Owen, Ursula (ed.), (1983) *Fathers: Reflections by Daughters* (London: Virago).

Phillips, A. (1994) *On Flirtation* (London: Faber & Faber).

Pilgrim, David (1997) 'Shrink Rapp and Shrink Resistance', in *Changes Journal*, 15:4.

Pines, Dinora (1993) *A Woman's Unconscious Use of Her Body* (London: Virago).

Prodgers, A. (1986) 'Touch and Psychotherapy', *Changes Journal*, April.

Prodgers, A. (1991) 'On Hating the Patient', *British Journal of Psychotherapy*, 8.

Rogers, Carl (1967) *On Becoming a Person* (London: Constable).

Rogers, Carl (1975) *The Theory and Practice of Group Psychotherapy* (New York: Basic Books).

Rose, Jacqueline (2004) *On Not Being Able to Sleep* (London: Vintage Books).

Roth, Philip (2000) *The Human Stain* (London: Jonathan Cape).

Rowe, Dorothy (1997) *The Real Meaning of Money* (London: HarperCollins).

Rowe, Dorothy (2001) *Friends and Enemies: Our Need to Love and Hate* (London: HarperCollins).

Rycroft, C., Gorer, G., Storr, A., Wren-Lewis, J. and Lomas, P. (1970) *Psychoanalysis Observed* (London: Pelican Books).

Sands, Anna (2000) *Falling for Therapy* (Basingstoke: Palgrave Macmillan).

Scecsody, I. (1990) *Psychoanalytic Psychotherapy*, 4:3, pp. 245–61.

Segal, H. (1964) *Introduction to the Work of Melanie Klein* (London: Heinemann).

Smith, Barbara Fletchman (1993) 'Assessing the Difficulties for British Patients of Caribbean Origin on Being Referred for Psychoanalytic Psychotherapy', *British Journal of Psychotherapy*, 10:1.

Solzhenitsyn, Alexander (1973) *The Gulag Archipelago* (New York: Harper & Row).

Stones, Christopher (2003) 'I Am Not Your Friend: I Am Your Therapist', *Journal of Critical Psychology, Counselling and Psychotherapy*, 3:4.

Storr, Anthony (1979) *The Art of Psychotherapy* (London: Secker & Warburg).

Sutherland, Stuart (1976) *Breakdown* (London: Weidenfeld & Nicolson).

Sullivan, Harry Stack (1953) *The Interpersonal Theory of Psychiatry* (New York: W. W. Norton).

Tallis, Frank (2002) 'Hidden Minds: a History of the Unconscious', *West Midlands Journal of Psychotherapy*, 20.

Tennatt, Alison (2003) 'Where Angels Fear to Tread: an Experience of Therapy', *Critical Journal of Psychology, Counselling and Psychotherapy*.

Tillett, R. (1998) 'Therapeutic Aggression', *British Journal of Psychotherapy*, 2.

Totton, N. (1997) 'Not Just a Job: Psychotherapy as a Spiritual and Political Practice'. In: R. House and N. Totton (eds), *Implausible Professions* (Ross on Wye: PCCS Books).

Winnicott, D. W. (1958) *Collected Papers* (London: Tavistock).

Yalom, Irvine D. (1975) *The Theory and Practice of Group Psychotherapy* (New York: Basic Books).

Index